MODELS FOR DIVINE ACTIVITY

MODELS FOR
Divine Activity

IAN T. RAMSEY
Bishop of Durham

WIPF & STOCK · Eugene, Oregon

Wipf and Stock Publishers
199 W 8th Ave, Suite 3
Eugene, OR 97401

Models for Divine Activity
By Ramsey, Ian T.
Copyright©1973 SCM-Canterbury Press Ltd
ISBN 13: 978-1-61097-258-1
Publication date 5/1/2011
Previously published by SCM Press, 1973

FOR MARGARET

CONTENTS

INTRODUCTION

The Zenos Lectures were established through the initiative of alumni of McCormick Theological Seminary, Chicago, in memory of Dean Andrew C. Zenos, a member of the McCormick faculty from 1891 until 1934, to enable outstanding scholars to lecture on some vital area of theological study.

Professor Ian Ramsey was invited in 1964 to give the Zenos Lectures in 1965, but it was not until March 1966 that the lectures could be delivered.

It had been hoped to transcribe the lectures from tape-recordings made at the time but, in the event, this did not prove possible. Mrs Shaw, Professor Ramsey's secretary in Oxford, was, however, able to produce a typescript from the original long-hand notes. Parts of the lectures were used and reused in discussions with students and clergy, in the years following the move from the Nolloth Professorship at Oxford to the See of Durham.

Bishop Ramsey went on hoping that the lectures would soon be published but, at the time of his death in October 1972, he had neither finished worrying at the wording nor revised the text to his satisfaction.

The lectures are, therefore, published in a form which many may find tantalizing. It is, however, to be hoped that both the questions and the way in which they are handled here will provoke and stimulate further discussion, and it may be that even the unrevised obscurities contribute to this.

Auckland Castle,   Harry McClatchey
Easter 1973

I

A New Perspective on the Doctrine of the Spirit: Models for Activity

As everyone knows, theology is at present in turmoil; and if I were asked to characterize our present discontents, I think I would select two features as basic to the present scene. First, there is the loss of a sense of God's presence; and secondly, there is a growing inability to see the point of theological discourse. We have become – for whatever reasons – insensitive to God; and theology – not God – has died on us. Theology seems often to the outsider just so much word-spinning, air-borne discourse which never touches down except disastrously. Not that this state of affairs is altogether new. George Berkeley in an earlier day criticized the 'abstracted metaphysics' which led to theological 'wire-drawing', and pointed to a broadened empiricism as the cure.

Can there be in our own day an empirical approach which could help to revitalize theological discourse: at one and the same time help people to see the point of theology and restore their vision of things unseen and eternal, in things seen and temporal? I am confident that there can, and that the recipe centres upon the twin themes of what I call models and disclosures – but that is to anticipate.

At least you see the background concerns which, with you, I bring to these lectures. Rather than generalize, I thought it best to take, by way of illustration, some specific theme. I shall illustrate my approach by taking some features of discourse about the Holy Spirit, to see if we can trace logical pathways through what often seems to be a veritable jungle. I begin with a quotation:

I have even heard clergymen say that they find Whit Sunday the hardest
of all the Church festivals to preach upon. If so, I think it shows, among
other things, that we very easily let our distinctively religious thought get
detached in a very disastrous fashion from our ordinary thought.[1]

So remarked William Temple in a memorable mission to the
University of Oxford some thirty years ago; and no doubt
Temple's remark was meant to explain the undoubted truth that
Whitsunday of all the festivals should clearly proclaim the
vitality, relevance and significance of the Christian faith. More
easily and obviously than any other doctrine, that of the Holy
Spirit should communicate vision and faith; of all doctrines it
should savour least of theological word-spinning and extrava-
gance.

And yet, on the other side, we are bound to admit that its
basis in the Bible seems variegated and diffuse to the point of
bewilderment; it might even seem as if there was not necessarily
anything specifically Christian about it, for at first sight the Old
Testament, as much as the New, abounds in references to the
Spirit. Further, we may think that in the early history of Christian
doctrine, it was the very success which attended the use of the
Logos concept to interpret the person of Jesus that led through
confusion and over-simplification to a neglect of the doctrine of
the Holy Spirit, until the rise of the heresy called Macedonian-
ism led to its being given a comparatively summary treatment in
the fourth century. So William Temple's clergymen might well
have found something to say by way of defence. Its scriptural
basic is very variegated; its doctrinal history relatively scant.

But the challenge behind Temple's remark remains: can we
then do anything at least to bring some order into the biblical
diversity, and at the same time to give the doctrine the lively
relevance it should have? The doctrine of the Holy Spirit, where
above all places Christian discourse should come alive to make
its point, seems particularly tangled and tortuous. Can we do
anything about it? In this lecture I shall only be concerned with
a preliminary question: what can we do to trace some pathways,
logical and theological, through discourse about the Spirit?

Let us begin by reminding ourselves that the word 'Spirit',
whether it be the Hebrew *ruach* or the Greek *pneuma* or the Latin
spiritus, originally meant a movement of air, wind or breath. So
the leading question, on the approach I am commending to you,

is: under what conditions does a movement of air, wind or breath become a *model* for God, when we could then become articulate about God in terms of the spirit? Alternatively, this is to ask for occasions when a wind gives rise to a 'cosmic disclosure', a situation when a wind reveals God. Of these occasions I shall distinguish two; and first we consider a gale.

Recall Joseph Conrad's description of the gale in 'Typhoon'. Captain MacWhirr is with his assistant, Jukes: and our extract begins with a reference to Jukes.

From the first stir of the air felt on his cheek the gale seemed to take upon itself the accumulated impetus of an avalanche. Heavy sprays enveloped the *Nan-Shan* from stem to stern, and instantly in the midst of her regular rolling she began to jerk and plunge as though she had gone mad with fright. . .

Captain MacWhirr . . . was trying to see, with that watchful manner of a seaman who stares into the wind's eye as if into the eye of an adversary, to penetrate the hidden intention and guess the aim and force of the thrust. The strong wind swept at him out of a vast obscurity; he felt under his feet the uneasiness of his ship, and he could not even discern the shadow of her shape. He wished it were not so; and very still he waited, feeling stricken by a blind man's helplessness. . .

The darkness palpitated down upon all this, and then the real thing came at last. It was something formidable and swift, like the sudden smashing of a vial of wrath. It seemed to explode all round the ship with an overpowering concussion and a rush of great waters, as if an immense dam had been blown up to windward. In an instant the men lost touch with each other. This is the disintegrating power of a great wind: it isolates one from one's kind. An earthquake, a landslip, an avalanche, overtake a man incidentally, as it were without passion. A furious gale attacks him like a personal enemy, tries to grasp his limbs, fastens upon his mind, seeks to rout his very spirit out of him.

Jukes was driven away from his commander. He fancied himself whirled a great distance through the air. Everything disappeared – even, for a moment, his power of thinking; but his hand had found one of the rail-stanchions. His distress was by no means alleviated by an inclination to disbelieve the reality of this experience. . . Moreover, the conviction of not being utterly destroyed returned to him through the sensations of being half-drowned, bestially shaken, and partly choked. . .

After a crushing thump on his back he found himself suddenly afloat and borne upwards. His first irresistible notion was that the whole China Sea had climbed on the bridge. Then, more sanely, he concluded himself gone overboard. All the time he was being tossed, flung, and rolled in great volumes of water, he kept on repeating mentally, with the utmost precipitation, the words: 'My God! My God! My God! My God!' . . .

When she rolled she fell on her side headlong, and she would be righted back by such a demolishing blow that Jukes felt her reeling as a clubbed man reels before he collapses. The gale howled and scuffled about gigantically in the darkness, as though the entire world were one black gully. . .

The *Nan-Shan* was being looted by the storm with a senseless, destructive fury: trysails torn out of the extra gaskets, double-lashed awnings blown away, bridge swept clean, weather-cloths burst, rails twisted, light-screens smashed – and two of the boats had gone already. They had gone unheard and unseen, melting, as it were, in the shock and smother of the wave. It was only later, when upon the white flash of another high sea hurling itself amidships, Jukes had a vision of two pairs of davits leaping black and empty out of the solid blackness, with one overhauled fall flying and an ironbound block capering in the air, that he became aware of what had happened within about three yards of his back.

He poked his head forward, groping for the ear of his commander. His lips touched it – big, fleshy, very wet. He cried in an agitated tone, 'Our boats are going now, sir.'

And again he heard that voice, forced and ringing feebly, but with a penetrating effect of quietness in the enormous discord of noises, as if sent out from some remote spot of peace beyond the black wastes of the gale; again he heard a man's voice – the frail and indomitable sound that can be made to carry an infinity of thought, resolution and purpose, that shall be pronouncing confident words on the last day, when heavens fall, and justice is done – again he heard it, and it was crying to him, as if from very, very far – 'All right.'[2]

A gale – awesome indeed; and my claim is that in and around the gale occurred a cosmic disclosure; a situation which takes on depth, to disclose another dimension, a situation where I am confronted in principle with the whole universe, a situation where God reveals himself. My belief is that Conrad told the story so as to give it disclosure possibilities. And I am supported in that belief first by the patently theological overtones of the language with which my extract concluded. Next, by phrases it contained such as: a vial of wrath; a rush of great waters; a header into a void; a strong wind swept out of a vast obscurity; as though the entire world were one black gully. But thirdly, by what Conrad himself wrote in *A Personal Record* some six or seven years later, where he compares his literary struggles with those of sailors who face the 'sombre stress of the westward winter passage round Cape Horn', and characterizes both as 'the wrestling of men with the might of their Creator, in a great isolation from the world, without the amenities and consolations of life, a lonely struggle under a sense of over-matched littleness, for no reward that could be adequate, but for the mere winning of a longitude . . .'³

Here were Captain MacWhirr and Jukes finding in the gale a loneliness, an isolation, a helplessness, and then finding in human dialogue an infinity of peace, resolution and purpose coming from some remote spot beyond. MacWhirr's words were indeed the Word of God. We may recall the wrestling of Jacob at the ford of Jabbok in Gen. 32, and the might of a Creator which was there disclosed to him. Again, loneliness, struggle, blessing.

Here is a situation leading to a disclosure of God, and then to discourse about God developed in the context of a gale, wind, and so providing us with specimen discourse about Spirit.

But when the biblical writers spoke of Spirit, it was no doubt the winds of their own land which they took as models. There were winds which, in their destructive discord, may be somewhat compared with Conrad's typhoon. These were the winds of which the term SherKiyeh, or Sirocco, was used. They are, we are told, hot winds, coming 'with a mist of fire sand, veiling the sun, scorching vegetation, and bringing languor and fever to men. They are most painful airs, and if the divine economy were only for our physical benefit, inexplicable, for they neither carry rain nor help at harvest.'⁴

But like Conrad's gale these winds could yield disclosure situations when the world took on depth and came alive in all its awfulness, even becoming like a personal enemy: grasping a man's limbs, fastening on his mind, routing out his spirit. From such a situation men spoke of God as mysterious, at least in a puzzling incomprehensible sense, invisible, powerful, whose 'breath' – whose 'spirit' – withereth the grass and fadeth the flower. . . Here was the Spirit of God contrasted in its power with the finitude and transitoriness of men.

But there were other winds in Palestine, those from the west, which were altogether kindlier. These, with the help of the sea, George Adam Smith tells us, fulfil two great functions throughout the year.

In the winter the west and southwest winds, damp from the sea, as they touch the cold mountains, drop their moisture and cause the winter rains. . . In summer the winds blow chiefly out of the drier north-west, and meeting only warmth do not cause showers, but greatly mitigate the daily heat. This latter function is even more regular than the former, for it is fulfilled morning by morning with almost perfect punctuality. Those who have not travelled through a Syrian summer can scarcely realise how welcome, how unfailing a friend is the forenoon wind from the sea, how he is strongest just after noon, and does not leave you till the need for his freshness passes away with the sunset. . . The peasants do their winnowing against this steady wind, and there is no happier scene in the land than afternoon on the threshing-floors, when he rustles the thickly-strewn sheaves, and scatters the chaff before him.[5]

Here are winds which 'greatly mitigate the daily heat'; which help people, which give them life, refresh and revitalize them, renew their activity, promote happiness.

Here is a situation where, feeling the cool wind blowing against their bodies and faces, men again breathed freely, came alive once more. Here is another situation when subjectively and objectively the world came alive and a wind which spoke of God also brought newness of life, new vitality, fellowship and happiness to man. Here is a situation where man comes alive spontaneously, where he affirms himself in an active response which is inspired, called forth, nurtured and constantly renewed by the activity of God. Here is another cosmic disclosure, and it supplies us again with the model of wind: licensing discourse of God in terms of breath, Spirit, of that which is always a criterion of personal existence. Of the man, injured in a road accident, we say: Is he breathing? Is he alive?

What our examples have shown is that from those particular situations which disclose God whose key-feature is wind, men were articulate about God in terms of Spirit and about themselves in terms of power, infinite assurance, blessing, vitality, fullness of life, fellowship, happiness.

But their own breath was in itself a movement of air; they, too, could blow and puff like the wind. So they, too, could speak of their power and fullness of life in terms of the spirit. It was when the Queen of Sheba was exhausted by Solomon's wisdom, not to say his food, and servants, clothing, cup-bearers and burnt offering, that it could be said that there was no spirit left in her.

You may object that all this is very familiar, that I am saying no more than what countless believers have said for centuries. In one obvious sense that is true. But what I am trying to do is not to invent new discourse but to trace logical paths through long-flourishing theological discourse and to point to an approach to the doctrine of the Holy Spirit, in particular. If my pathways are so far reliable, 'spirit' is the name for no 'thing': rather have we to say that *discourse about the Spirit is a way of being articulate about God's initiating activity and our responsive activity, and it is a way which is licensed by, as it originates in, situations where God discloses himself in occasions characterized by wind and gales.* This is where the logical origin of talk about the Spirit is to be found, and whenever we can speak of Jesus in terms of Spirit it is because the situations in which men found themselves with him had echoes of the situations in which they have known the revitalizing, powerful effects of the wind. Jesus situations and wind situations were isomorphous.

Let me illustrate generally some implications of this view by reference to two areas where theological problems all too easily arise: talk of God as Creator Spirit, and talk of an indwelling Spirit.

A.   With the model of the bracing wind as the giver of life and with breathing as a criterion of life, discourse about the Spirit leads to talk of God as Creator. I am suggesting that it is such a model of the bracing wind which gives rise to phrases such as these: in Gen. 2.7, 'The Lord God breathed into men's nostrils the breath of life'; in Gen. 6.17, where we read of 'flesh in which is the spirit/breath of life'; in Rev. 11.11, which speaks of 'the breath of life from God' which enables the two prophets to stand on their feet again; and gives rise to such stories as we have in Ezek. 37 – the well-known story of the valley of dry bones. Now if the logical status of the discourse goes unrecognized, and its origins in the model of wind are forgotten, it might be supposed that this was sheer anthropomorphism married to the crudest possible biology. Whereas what these assertions are saying is rather that all our life and all our activity derive from the existence and activity of God. Talk of the Lord God breathing into us the breath of life is *talk whose point will not be appreciated until it has been grounded in that kind of situation* of mutually matching activities which occurs when we experience a bracing wind. This is a *sine qua non* of our grasping the point of the theological discourse about the Creator Spirit. Alternatively expressed, we cannot possibly appreciate Gen. 2.7 unless we know for ourselves, first-hand or imaginatively, situations like those known to the dwellers in Palestine and to Conrad.

Further, let us notice that when doctrines of creation, to take our present example, developed from this model of wind originating in a disclosure situation, they were appealing to situations recognizable in principle by the secular world. Here was no word-spinning, airborne theology. Further, it always pointed up a sense of mystery and transcendence. For as there is always something mysterious and elusive about the wind – the example of the gale and the struggle of Jacob provide us with paradigms – so also with the spirit. We may recall the well-known *logion* in the Fourth Gospel: 'The wind blows where it will and you hear the sound of it, but you do not know whence it comes or whither it goes – so is everyone born of the Spirit' (John 3.8); as you know, the one word can just as well be translated 'wind' or 'spirit'. The same mystery of the spirit can be found in Eccles. 11.5: 'You do not know how the Spirit comes to the bones in the womb of a woman with child', so, 'you do not know the work of God who makes everything'. It is true that in the days of weather ships and coastal patrols we can say much more about a wind than once was possible, 'whence it comes: whither it goes'. But there is still a sense in which we do not know whence it comes or whither it goes: the gale, the Sirocco, the west winds can still point to God and license discourse about mystery and transcendence.

So talk about God breathing into men's nostrils, which may seem at best crude anthropomorphism; and talk about a Creator Spirit which seems to so many of our contemporaries vacuous theology – all such misunderstandings receive each its corrective when it is recognized that all such discourse derives from a model of wind which arises as a constituent part of a disclosure situation, and that it is in a situation of this kind, arising in this way, that a defence of this theological discourse about Spirit is finally to be found.

B.   Let me take as a second illustration talk of an indwelling spirit, which seems to many a dangerously pantheistic way of talking. Obviously the model of breath and wind makes it logically possible to talk and think of breath as indwelling wind, or wind as an all-pervading breath; so that if the model were thought of as providing a descriptive picture, pantheism could hardly be avoided. But the word 'indwelling' seen as associated with wind or breath points rather to that inwardness which characterizes our breathing; reminds us that God's initiative and our response concerns our inmost selves; that God finds us, if so you like to express it, in 'depth'. My point is that rightly to understand phrases such as 'indwelling' when used of the spirit, we must first in principle reconstitute the model and the dis-closure situation of which it is an essential part. If we do this, we can see how talk of indwelling spirit is rather talk of God's active initiative, and our response being known in the very depths, the deep inwardness of our being. In short, here is the logical origin of discourse about the Spirit which talks of inspiration, and inti-mate fellowship. For inspiration is what happens when we are stirred to a self-disclosure which reveals each of us as more than the overt behaviour which in plain fact we are. Inspiration is what stirs us, as it could be said, to the depths of our being, and in this way reveals that to which the word 'I' characteristically refers. Or, to speak more accurately, when we use the word 'I' in genuine first-person utterances, we use language performatively as currency for our self-disclosing activity as it occurs.

So it is that 'spirit' refers, subjectively speaking, to what is characteristically personal: wisdom, and moral virtues, the spirit of wisdom and understanding, the spirit of counsel, inward strength, the spirit of knowledge and of the fear of the Lord. So it is, too, that we speak of what is most characteristically our-selves, that in which our true subjectivity is realized, as the 'spiritual'; to do most justice to what is distinctive about a human being we speak of 'the spirit' rather than of 'minds' or 'bodies'.

My claim then is that talk about the 'spirit' has to be construed as model talk about God's *activity* and about our own, i.e. as discourse which has been derived from and is spelt out in terms of the model of wind or breath when this is used to be articulate about a cosmic disclosure.

In the next section I would like to take these ideas a little further, and I will do this by first asking the question: *Cannot this activity of God and ourselves meeting in a disclosure situation be explicated in terms of other models?* Undoubtedly, as I shall show, it can. In that case, and if my contention were reliable, it would not be surprising if these other models give rise to discourse which becomes interwoven with discourse about spirit. It is this multi-model character of theological discourse which gives it its luxurious, not to say lush, character, but it also generates prob-lems for logical sorting which are not solved until the complex, multi-model character of the discourse is displayed.

However, let us take some examples of other models for God's activity and see how these models have been associated with discourse about the spirit. First: fire. With the awesomeness of a gale may be compared that of a volcanic eruption, and the fire and smoke and heat and lava coming from Mount Sinai must have been a terrifying spectacle. We may recall Ex. 19.16: 'And it came to pass on the third day, when it was morning, that there were thunders and lightnings, and a thick cloud upon the mount . . . and Mount Sinai was altogether on smoke, because the Lord descended upon it in fire. . .' The basis for such assertions is, I suggest, a cosmic disclosure around the volcano, and in particular around the fire; around the fire, the whole universe came alive, the situation took on depth, another dimension, an infinite dimension. . . The Lord descended upon it in fire – God active. . . God confronting Moses, and Moses actively responded to God's initiative. 'The Lord came down upon Mount Sinai (v. 20) and Moses went up.'

With fire and spirit as models for God's activity it is not surprising that discourse about fire and discourse about spirit are interwoven as in Isa. 4.4: the bloodstains of Jerusalem would be cleansed 'by the *spirit* of *burning*'; and there is the well-known phrase in Ps. 104.4: 'Who maketh his angels spirits and his ministers a flame of fire'; or 'Who maketh thy messengers spirits, fire and flame thy ministers.'

Secondly, we may take the example of anointing: an activity practised in response to a claim discerned as bearing on men. We may take as a paradigm the familiar story of the call of David. Of Jesse's sons Eliab, Abinadab, Shammah and in turn all the seven passed before Samuel. But there was no disclosure. No light dawned. The situation remained flat, bleak, uninspiring, despite the impressive physical features of the sons. There had been no 'deeper' impact; nothing heart-warming, heart-felt. So often man looks on the outward appearance, doesn't 'see' beyond the surface: there is no depth, no extra dimension. Then came David. The situation took on depth. Heart spoke to heart. God disclosed himself: 'This is he.' A cosmic demand impressed itself on Samuel through David as it impressed itself on Brigham Young through the plains of Utah, and the anointing was symbolic of the response of both Samuel and David to the God who disclosed himself. Samuel took the horn of oil, and anointed him

(David) in the midst of his brethren: and we read, 'the spirit of the Lord came mightily upon David from that day forward'. We could offer as logical translations: God's powers were active in and through David; God dwelt actively in David; but then we may also recall the conjunction of these two models in the parallelism of Isa. 61.1: 'The Spirit of the Lord is upon me because the Lord hath anointed me.'

Thirdly, God's activity was seen in the rain and in the dew. In Hos. 6.3: 'He shall come unto us as the rain, as the latter rain that watereth the earth', or Hos. 14.4f.: 'I will love them. . . I will be as the dew unto Israel.' The dew in the heat of harvest, the showers that water the earth: these were occasions of cosmic disclosures. In and through the dew and the showers, God disclosed himself as active, and man responded in thankful work.

Once again, it is significant for my argument that discourse about rain and discourse about the spirit can be found interwoven, as in Isa. 44.3: 'For I will pour water upon him that is thirsty and streams upon the dry ground: I will pour my spirit upon thy seed, and my blessing upon thine offspring'; and we recall that when the Spirit was mentioned in Gen. 1, it was a spirit which moved on the face of the waters.

I have argued then that discourse about the Spirit is a way of being articulate about the activity of God, a way which, while it derives primarily from situations containing the model of wind or breath, is also intertwined and cross-woven with discourse originating in the models of fire, rain and dew, water and oil. So the activity of God can be spoken of in terms of wind and breath and life, telling of mystery and power; it can be said, like water and rain and dew, to refresh and cleanse and purify and revive; like oil, it can soothe and illuminate: and some words, e.g. 'revive', occur in more than one strand of discourse. But all this only serves to make it clear that here we have *not models* for *Spirit*, but that *Spirit* itself, as synonymous with wind or breath, is a *model*, for that which all the models presuppose, and which all the models elucidate, viz. God's *activity*. It happens to be a further complication that in English, when God is reached in any of these ways, the word Spirit is often used as a logical synonym of 'God active'. Which only goes to show what a logically complex discourse we are trying to construe.

I will conclude with two other points, the first of which highlights from another point the logical complexity of our exercise. We have noticed already that the word 'indwelling' has been used to relate the Spirit of God to the Spirit of man, when, and because, a bracing wind restores our vitality, brings us to ourselves inwardly, stirs us deeply. Now the liquid models of oil and water can easily and obviously give rise to discourse about pouring and filling: hence we have phrases like the pouring out of the spirit, and being filled with the spirit. Further, such phrases are sometimes linked with the word 'indwelling' when this is interpreted in terms of a receptacle-like background picture, so that there is the picture of a receptacle in which the spirit is poured like a fluid.

To add to misunderstanding here, Spirit itself, and quite independently, came to have a fluid context when and because of the fluid which was supposed to run in the human body: 'animal spirits'; and it was 'spirits' which when drunk made people behave in strange ways. Plainly, this could become associated, as I have said, with very crude talk about an indwelling spirit, and I fear that it is this fluid and receptacle context which is so often the popular setting for phrases like 'being filled with the Spirit', and God's 'pouring out' the Spirit. But this is to have a theology of the Spirit which is nothing but a crass materialism. It is to disfranchise talk of the Spirit by using discourse which has no relation to a cosmic disclosure, but is only plain, flat, descriptive. It is only fair to add that J. E. Yates believes this to be the original context, even if misguided.[6] I grant it is an ancient context, one which, in the case of the drunken man, might have been associated with awesome fear. It is also one which might once have seemed to be scientific. But it can have few attractions today. Rather must we contextualize these phrases, e.g. 'pouring' and 'filling', in such a way that they talk more clearly of an activity rather than a commodity, and of subjective inwardness rather than an inner receptacle. Let us think of 'pour out' rather as the verb used of the pouring out of wine when the vessel burst, and so for the pouring out of money or blood: a generous outpouring which can be taken metaphorically as a bestowal. Similarly, 'to be filled with' is better contextualized in such a way as to speak of being richly furnished with, to abound in, as for example we read in I Kings 7.14 that Hiram of Tyre was filled with wisdom, understanding and skill for making any work in bronze.

So we could speak of the Spirit being poured out, or of someone filled with the Spirit, when the bestowal of the Spirit was the bestowal of intellectual or moral gifts, and when to abound in the Spirit was to be richly furnished with (say) wisdom and skills. In this way we have another illustration of the importance of what has been the central theme of this lecture, viz.: *never let our discourse about the Spirit get too distant from a cosmic disclosure where God and ourselves meet in an active interchange,* the cosmic disclosure in which the discourse must finally be anchored.

My second point illustrates how with discourse about the Spirit, when it is rightly construed, there can be empirical criteria for its appraisal. When we are articulate about the Spirit from models such as we have suggested, empirical fit becomes possible; and it is not a pseudo-scientific verification which the fluid context for Spirit might lead us to suppose. Rather does it arise like this. Those who are filled with the Spirit, those who act 'spiritually', those who fulfil themselves because of the active influence of God, are those who display genuine wisdom, 'humane behaviour' as distinct from routine, impersonal behaviour, a moral stature which is more than just rectitude. In so far as these empirical distinctions are possible, they point back to the kind of situation it is the function of language about the Spirit to elucidate. To understand the doctrine of the Spirit, then, my large-scale recommendation is: translate assertions about the Spirit in terms of activity, whether of God or man; and to recapture the situations which justify this talk of activity, go back to the models which point to the cosmic disclosures which are the empirical anchorage for all our talk about God.

What pathways, then, have I tried to trace in an endeavour to approach the doctrine of the Holy Spirit from a new direction? My first point was that discourse about the Spirit is a way of being articulate about God's initiating activity and our responsive activity, which originate when God discloses himself in situations – cosmic disclosures, I called them – characterized by wind and gales; that talk of a Creator Spirit or of an 'indwelling Spirit' is only rightly construed when it is analysed as talk whose point will not be appreciated until it has recreated for us precisely the kind of situation which occurs around a bracing wind, when we are revitalized, when we come alive, realize ourselves.

But we then asked: cannot this activity bear other models? We showed how the models of fire, anointing and water are used in this way. It supported my overall point that we do not here have models for Spirit, but that *Spirit*, like wind or breath, is a model for that which all the models presuppose and which all the models elucidate, viz. *God's activity*. This is the key-phrase in terms of which the doctrine of the Spirit, Holy Spirit, should be interpreted.

Finally, I illustrated my main point: never let our discourse about the Spirit get too distant from a cosmic disclosure where God and ourselves meet in an active interchange. I noted the gross errors that arise when the word Spirit is given nothing more than a fluid contextualization, and concluded by showing how a doctrine of the Spirit construed in this way can secure what I called empirical fit. But I repeat my main point. So as to bring some order into our doctrine of the Spirit I suggest that we take as our key-phrase *God's activity*. *Spirit is a noun* whose logical tradition is more reliably a verb: *being active, God-active*. It tells of a becoming, not a *being*; it is a vector whose logical character is often misunderstood as a scalar.

NOTES

1. William Temple, *Christian Faith and Life*, SCM Press [18]1963, p. 94.
2. Joseph Conrad, *Typhoon*, Chapter III.
3. Quoted in Gerard Jean-Aubry, *The Sea Dreamer*, Allen and Unwin 1957, a definitive biography of Joseph Conrad.
4. George Adam Smith, *The Historical Geography of the Holy Land*, Hodder and Stoughton 1894, p. 67.
5. Op. cit., pp. 66f.
6. See J. E. Yates, *The Spirit and the Kingdom*, S.P.C.K. 1963.

II

The Model of Economy

In my first lecture I tried to trace logical pathways in a particularly tough and complex area of Christian discourse so that negatively we might avoid certain theological crudities and blunders, and more positively that we might revitalize discourse which otherwise conceals what it is meant to talk of and to reveal. In this way, I suggested, we might restore a sense of God and give point to theological discourse, which at present often lacks it.

My second lecture is dedicated to the same end, but approaches it from a very different direction. Here we shall take a specimen of theological discourse which has virtually disappeared, and yet it originated in what, for those of us who are concerned to elucidate a relevant and lively theology, might have been thought to be the most promising use of a very secular model. This was the model of 'economy', *oikonomia*.

Let me begin then by reminding you that in the early days of the Christian church, the word 'economy' was not only used of God, but also had a well-recognized secular use. In the secular use, the verb 'to economize' meant to administer some group, e.g. a civic community, as Raymond Daly administers Chicago. By what logical route did this secular concept come to be used about God?

Put briefly, my answer falls into three stages.

1. 'Economy' in its secular use which told of some ordered administration, as distinct from chaos or even some *ad hoc* assemblage, succeeded by this very pattern in disclosing characteristically human activity. In and through the pattern of an

'economy' men were aware of the persons who gave that economy its pattern. I think you can see how patterns can disclose persons. If I look from a cliff on to a beach below, which to the best of my knowledge is inaccessible, I may see on the sand a haphazard array of stones, and nothing about them would strike me. They would stir no questions, arouse no wonder.

Suppose now we see an array of stones in a continuous wavy line. Something might strike us, demand our attention, stir us to ask questions, 'What caused the stones to fall into this pattern?', and these questions might be answered in terms of the tidal currents, the shelving of the beach, the size of the pebbles and so on. In this way the pattern of stones would be set in a progressively larger pattern of causal antecedents, and the way prepared for a cosmic disclosure of the kind I shall have in mind in the next lecture. But for our present purpose this is irrelevant, for the visible pattern in no way discloses a person. By contrast, suppose the array of stones now makes up a more intricate pattern of regular recurrences: say a cross followed by a circle repeated twenty-five times. Again something strikes us, demands our attention, but this time we can say, 'The beach isn't inaccessible – persons are there.' Here is a pattern disclosing a person; and to get back to my original concern, the pattern of an 'economy' in a similar way disclosed the person who ordered it.

2.   If 'economy' is to be used in relation to God, there must be features of such a secular 'economy', features of this pattern that are isomorphous with features of the universe – in other words, there must in both cases be regular recurrences.

3.   The human secular case then acts as a catalyst for the divine case, so that when certain regular patterns – night and day, seed-time and harvest – are seen to characterize the universe, a cosmic disclosure occurs around them. Whereupon God (if we may use the word God without further ado for the objective reference of the disclosure – a point to which I will return in the last lecture), disclosing himself in the cosmic disclosure, is spoken of in discourse deriving from 'economy' as a model.

It is very important, however, that we do not misunderstand the logic of this answer. It must *not* be construed as a plain argument from analogy, or else we have to face all the problems and embarrassments of David Hume's treatment of the argument from design. It is interesting indeed to recall that Hume himself uses the concept of 'economy' pejoratively in relation to the argument from design when in Part II of his *Dialogues concerning Natural Religion* he criticizes those who use this argument, as being far worse than a peasant who 'makes his domestic economy the rule for the government of Kingdoms'. 'Economy' as a model offers no straight analogy, it must rather encourage a way of looking at the world, which leads in the way I have suggested to a cosmic disclosure; to a God who may disclose himself at some point as we develop a particular perspective on the universe.

But the logical functions of models are not exhausted by pointing to the cosmic disclosures in which they find their fulfilment. Models must enable us to be theologically articulate, and for this desired discourse there must be the possibility of some sort of empirical fit. Taking the model of economy as our illustration, we will now elaborate each of these two functions of models.

First, then, how does the model of economy enable us to be theologically articulate? To answer that question let us look at three non-theological, secular uses of the word:

The first relates to administration, and I quote from G. L. Prestige, *God in Patristic Thought.*

Oikonomeō means primarily to administer or oversee an office, such as a bishopric or a civil community (*hom. Clem.* 3.60; Ath. *c. Gent.* 43). Then it covers the administration of property; canon 26 of the Council of Chalcedon directs every church possessing a bishop to maintain also a treasurer, chosen from its own clergy, to 'economise' or administer the ecclesiastical property in accordance with the bishop's instructions. In this last sense it appears absolutely, meaning 'to be treasurer' (Chrysostom on *St. John* 65.2: 'Why indeed did He entrust to one who was a thief the treasury of the poor, or cause a covetous person to "economise"?'). Next, it means to regulate or control in a general sense, as the natural forces of the body '*economise*' the functions of animal life (Bas. *de ieiunio* 1.4), or as spiritual beings 'economise' their life on selective and prudent principles.[1]

This leads naturally to the second context where economy is contextualized in discourse about discipline. Prestige continues:

From this usage the word comes to be applied to the penitential system in particular, meaning in the active 'administer penance', and in the passive 'be subjected to penance', as in Greg. Nyss. *ep. can.* 4 (Migne 45.229B), where it is stated that the person *administering* ecclesiastical *discipline* may shorten the time of penance in suitable cases, or Bas. *ep.* 217 *can.* 72, which directs that a person guilty of consulting diviners shall be *disciplined* for the same period as if for homicide.

There is then a third context where economy relates to the making of provision to meet cases of need.

On the other hand, it also means to 'dispense' alms to recipients (*apost. const.* 2.25.2), and to 'supply' with the necessaries of life: instead of, 'Your heavenly Father feedeth them' (*Matt.* vi.26), the *Acts of Thomas* (28) paraphrases with 'God economises them', and pseudo-Macarius remarks, *hom.* 12.14, 'he was nourished by God and his body was economised with other celestial food'.

Prestige concludes:

The prevailing ideas, so far, are those of administration and provision for need,

but we may add what he, rather surprisingly, omits: 'and discipline'.

It is because it integrates these three areas of discourse that the model for economy gives rise to discourse about providence, and Prestige remarks:

A word with such a range of associations was extremely apt for adoption as an expression of the providential order. It covers either such gifts as God sends and supplies in a providential manner, or such events as He designs and disposes.[2]

Further, an administrator not only exercises a broad over-arching control, he pays attention to particular needs. Indeed, the 'economy' closest to the derivation of the word – *oikonomia*, 'the ordering of a household' – is precisely one where over-all provision incorporates the meeting of particular needs. Hence the model of economy not only makes possible talk of a providential order in general, it also makes possible talk of a *particular* providence. The early Christian had no hesitation about speaking in this way. As Prestige remarks:

The treatment of the subject would be incomplete without illustrating the ascription to 'economy' of particular instances of a dispensation of mercy or special divine interposition.[3]

More broadly, we might say, the concepts of 'dispensation' and 'covenant' both presuppose a specially-directed, a particularly-intentioned activity. Prestige himself gives us many illustrations. For example:

Justin (*dial.* 107.3) calls the growth of the gourd to shelter Jonah from the heat an economy, and . . . such economy of God was experienced by Dionysius of Alexandria (ap. Eus. *h. e.* 7.11.2) in the course taken by his own trial before the deputy-prefect. 'Lo, by economy of God they met a donkey-driver,' is the phrase employed in the *Acts of Xanthippe and Polyxena* (31); and Eusebius (*h. e.* 2.1.13) asserts that an economy led the eunuch from the land of the Ethiopians to Philip. Elsewhere (*ib.* 2.2.6) he makes the remark, 'The heavenly providence by economy put this into his head'; and again (*mart. Pal.* 11.28), ascribes to an economy of the providence of God the fact that the bodies of certain martyrs were not harmed by wild beasts, but were preserved for Christian burial. The apostles, according to Cyril of Jerusalem (*cat.* 15.4), were moved by divine purpose according to economy to address a question to our Lord.[4]

Gregory of Nazianzus ascribes the sufferings he endured to an economy.

So, too, Chrysostom regarded St. Paul's conversion as an economy (on *Eph.* 6.2), and states (on *St. Matt.* 9.3) that God is accustomed to fulfil His own economies even through His adversaries' action. The monks in the desert had as strong a sense of the detailed guidance and overruling of events as had the Fathers in their studies. 'God did us this economy,' says one of them in the *apophthegmata patrum* (*Abb. Mac.* 2), 'that neither do we freeze in winter nor does the heat do us injury in summer.' 'By economy it became dusk' says another (*ib., Eul. presb.*). 'By economy of God the old man went to those parts', remarks John Moschus (*prat. spir.* 83). God's hand was recognised in the smallest things as in the greatest.[5]

But let us notice already a point to which I shall return presently, that when God's hand *was* recognized in the smallest things, (i) they were contextualized widely and the resulting discourse never conflicted with a broader understanding of the universe; rather did it offer a more *detailed* interpretation e.g. of dusk and nightfall, and (ii) did not exclude suffering. For the early church particular providence was not always smiling like the families on our advertisement signs.

Undoubtedly, then, the articulation possibilities for this model are enormous; it combines the broad theme of an over-all providence, what is traditionally called 'general providence', including what Joseph Butler would have called the moral government of the world, with the theme of a God who is watchful over all our particular needs, a particular providence. Few models could be more prolific in their articulation possibilities.

Further, to turn to the second feature which is characteristic of a model, we can see how easily discourse deriving from the model of economy can, in principle, touch down on the world around us to be given, where it can, 'empirical fit'. In order to use this model not only to be articulate, which as I have said is easy, but to be *reasonably* articulate about God's providence, and about God's moral government of the world, the world must be such as to bear the discourse to which the model leads. Put more picturesquely, for the model of 'economy' to gain empirical fit, for the discourse it makes possible, it is a *sine qua non* that a hymn like Whittier's or Cowper's, or that of Tate and Brady, should ring true to experience. It must be the case

that blessings undeserved have marked my erring track
that care and trial have seemed at last through memory's sunset air
like mountain ranges over-past, in purple distance fair
that more and more a providence of love is understood
making the springs of time and sense – all that belongs
to our transitoriness and decay – sweet with eternal good.

It must be the case that the clouds we so much dreaded have been filled with unexpected blessings. Experience must have enabled us to decide how blest are they and only they who in his love confide. It must be the case that taking a long perspective on the events of our lives, on the fortunes of humanity generally, patterns of the kind which an 'economy' displays, patterns appropriate to the running of a household – for that, you recall, is what comes closest to the Greek word *oikonomia* – shall be able to be delineated. If the empirical circumstances were such that some threatening frowning state of affairs could rarely, if ever, be seen in the perspective of a world smiling upon us; if Whittier's counsel to take a long look back never showed cares and trials like mountain ranges overpast, never traced undeserved blessings, then providential discourse would be unjustified, and the model of economy virtually useless as a guide to the logic of Christian or theistic discourse. If the model of economy originated in a cosmic disclosure, we might have to believe in a Devil rather than in God, or at least in what Hume called 'mixed principles'. But let us not otherwise suppose that specifically Christian discourse derives from a model of 'economy' which is contextualized in terms of financial patronage or the most favoured nation treatment, still less which smacks of favouritism. The Christian model of economy, like the Christian household, is contextualized in love: which means that for empirical fit it must be possible to find patterns in the universe which can be 'interpreted by love'. To recall the examples of our first lecture, though the gale is 'like a personal enemy' and the Sirocco scorches vegetation and brings languor and fever to men, somehow some way we must be able to make our theological discourse fit them. For as George Adam Smith himself remarked, 'If the divine economy were only for our physical benefit', then events would be inexplicable. But it is precisely my present point that an economy of love may in principle incorporate them while the economy of immediate pleasurable benefits will miss them. For the way of love is not infrequently the way of suffering and a Cross. Not that we have grappled with all the difficulties even now. For, as we saw, to use the model of economy makes logically possible talk of a particular providence.

But, it might be asked, does not all talk of particular providence make the activity of God inevitably smack of favouritism? 'One man taken; another left.' Can we speak of the providence of God when of two riders on the covered wagon, one is killed by Indians and his companion goes unscathed? No. But what is wrong here is not the basic claim to discern God in particular events. What is wrong is the specific interpretation given to the events: an interpretation of such a kind that providence easily becomes synonymous with a 'lucky escape' or a 'happy chance', and indeed is in head-on collision with theism. Not that this is only an error of particular providence: it has often characterized doctrines of general providence as well. There have been those who thought of general providence being a dispensation for favourites! The epiglottis was that which saved aldermen at a City dinner from choking on every mouthful of turkey – splendid for the aldermen, but unfortunate for the turkeys. There is no limit to the absurdities which too narrow a view of providence can generate. Yet, *abusus non tollit usum*; the possibility of abuse must not compromise the possibility of use.

Certainly, as the early Fathers saw, the model of 'economy' and the talk about particular providence to which it can lead can be justified if, first, God be discerned in the way particular needs are met, and this will no doubt be the case if disclosures occur around certain particular arrangements of events – patterns, for example, like those which have generally been called 'miracles of coincidence'. When we are trying to restore to people a sense of

God, it would be ironic if we denied to them the possibility of discerning God around particular configurations of events in their lives. But, further, what we must at all costs ensure is that, secondly, what is then disclosed is talked of in a way which is reputable both in relation to what we wish to say elsewhere about God, and in its possibilities of empirical fit. If the man on the covered wagon speaks genuinely of the particular providence of God, his discourse about God must also incorporate the death of his friend. We are back with the wise caution about breadth of discourse and the need to incorporate suffering, of which I reminded you when we illustrated particular providence from the early Fathers. And let me remind you again that unless we are overwhelmed by the linguistic risks which a doctrine of particular providence involves, we shall not seek to deny to a generation which has lost the sense of God, the possibility of one range of patterns which may disclose it.

We have seen, then, how the model of economy can encourage the broad perspective. It can be set in a cosmic disclosure which talks of providence and the moral government of the world; but it can also talk of a cosmic disclosure which centres on a focal pattern of events. Alternatively expressed, it can speak of cosmic activity which is diffused throughout the universe; it can also speak of a cosmic activity which is nevertheless particularized at a point. It can speak of the mysteries of a general providence; it can also speak of the intimacy of a personal encounter. He who administers, exercises an over-all control, but he can still meet those he administers as a friend.

The moral I shall now draw is that this word economy – presiding over such a variegated discourse, with the possibilities of such wide empirical fit, and harmonizing the two strands of a 'general' and a 'particularized' activity – is, for these very reasons, a word whose logic is closely similar to that of the word of God itself, and it will be hardly surprising when we look at the use of the model economy in Christian discourse to find that, indeed, the word was used synonymously with the Trinity.

Before drawing to my conclusion, let me make one other point that eventually supports what I have said about a particular providence. As my discussion will, I hope, by implication have made clear, economy is a model which, like that of wind, or fire, or water, or oil, enables us to be articulate about a disclosed activity. Once again, as with discourse about the Spirit, it is 'activity' which is the assured datum in any disclosure; for in the cosmic disclosure we are aware of an activity disclosing itself, bearing on us – we are aware of being acted upon prior to our active response.

In this connection it is significant that Prestige can quote Maximus Confessor and remark:

> In Maximus Confessor economy becomes typical of one of three forms in which he recognises the expression of divine volition. 'We must assume three wills in God – that of purpose (*eudokia*), that of economy, and that of acquiescence (or concession)' (*quaest. et dub.* 20). He illustrates the first by the call of Abraham, the second by the ordering of Joseph's life towards the foreseen conclusion of his career, and the third by the trials of the patriarch Job.[6]

This reminds us that economy, like purpose or design, is but one model to talk about activity; that economy, like purpose, logically presupposes activity. Indeed, I think we can go further. Does not economy presuppose purpose, as perhaps administration presupposes economy? At any rate, in this possibility we have a glimpse of an ordered array of models such as often characterize theological discourse, and the relevance to our earlier discussion is this: that the more detailed our discourse is about God, the closer our model to the perimeter of the array, the more cautious we must be as we develop discourse from it. Discourse about God is the more reliable the less detailed it is: this is another reason why we should always develop a particular teleology with the maximum circumspection.

Economy then, as we have abundantly seen, functioned as a model, and confirmation that this is a reliable account of the logic which the word had in early Christian discussion may be found in an interesting if rather indirect way. If economy is a model, it will, like all models, carry the associated notion of a tentative approximation; it will also carry overtones of mystery; and it will be additionally helpful from the point of view of apologetic and evangelism if argument can start from where people are, if the model has a secular use. Making these same points from the opposite direction, if we wished to talk of a tentative theology, of the limitations of theological discourse, and to link them with the concept of mystery and to conduct a reasonable apologetic, the word 'economy' would carry with it the correct logical overtones. This of course would be the case logically with any model. The fact that of all possible models 'economy' was selected for this purpose implies that here, in this model, the limitations of theological discourse, its concern with mystery and its apologetic value were most clearly seen, and/or that this model was of all models the most popular. Certainly these were the three features specially associated with the word economy, and I can illustrate my contention with two phrases from Dr Bethune-Baker's *Introduction to the Early History of Christian Doctrine.*

In discussing the development of doctrine, Bethune-Baker contrasts 'the fidelity of the revelation in Christ' with 'the gradual process by which expression is found for the true interpretation of it'. Here, he remarks, is an 'economy' or 'accommodation', a sort of 'prudent ordering' of the truth which leads to a sense of theological reserve. Here is a sense in which theology is wisely tentative. As Bethune-Baker remarks:

> Language is, in any case, so inadequate to express the deepest thought and feeling on such questions, that it may well seem that if the true idea is secured it matters little in what precise language it is clothed. It is impossible to be certain that a particular term will convey the same idea to different people. The thing that matters is the idea.[7]

We may not ourselves wish to talk, as Bethune-Baker does, of securing 'the true idea' – but broadly we share his sentiments. But this brings me to the second point.

Here, too, is the foundation of a sense of mystery, for to recognise an economy about one's theology is to recognize something other than the theology which is being continuously economized – indeed the revelation of God in Jesus Christ. Revelation is to this degree mysterious. Bethune-Baker has much to say about the misuse:

> In controversy with opponents the truth might be stated in terms as acceptable as possible to them. It would always be right to point out as fully as possible how much of the truth was already implied, if not expressed, in the faith and religious opinions which were being combated. It would be right to shew that the new truth included all that was true in the old, and to state it as much as possible in the familiar phraseology: such *argumenta ad hominem* might be the truest and surest ways of enlightening an opponent. But phrases of some of the Alexandrian Fathers are cited which sound like undue extensions of such fair 'economy'. Clement

declared (*Strom.* vii 9) that the true Gnostic 'bears on his tongue whatever he has in his mind', but only 'to those who are worthy to hear', and adds that 'he both thinks and speaks the truth, unless at any time medicinally, as a physician dealing with those who are ill, for the safety of the sick he will lie or tell an untruth'.[8]

Further, we can now see how the principle of economy can be misused. It is misused if it is thought to license any way of talking whatever so long as that way of talking commends itself to your opponents – on the supposition that if the revelation is never adequately expressed by any language, then any old language might conceivably be saying something about it. May be. But it is not reasonable to make that claim unless it relates to articulation from some model or other which is grounded in a cosmic disclosure where God discloses himself even if he does not disclose the gospel. In this way the concept of models can help us to distinguish a legitimate appeal to the light that lighteth every man and so can be found even in those who were traditionally called 'benighted', and a way of talking which used language quite erroneously and was, as Bethune-Baker remarks, dangerous and dishonest.

But let me conclude as I began, and introduce my conclusion with a question: Why did 'economy' – a model with all these articulation possibilities – virtually disappear from theology, so much so that in Dr Cross's *Dictionary of the Christian Church* it does not even have an entry? The answer is: I do not know. Some might say it was because the Western approach edged out the Eastern approach – and theology became much more legalistic and precise, cut and dried, rather than more philosophical, more subtle, doing more justice to a sense of mystery. But whatever the reason, at least I am trying to rehabilitate the model – or am I? I suppose that rather am I trying to commend a model which has the same articulation possibilities and which is at the same time so much a part of secular life: and then I ask the question – is there any model today which might, in principle, fulfil these conditions? I cannot be sure, but if only as a possible exemplar, I think it is worth mentioning the model of 'depth'.

Here is a model which occurs in a vast variety of discourse. We speak of being deeply moved by a novel, a play; having a deep affection for a friend; having a deep concern for the social well-being of men and women whatever their creed or colour or class.

Further, as Bishop Robinson himself remarks, the word 'depth' is also characteristic of certain scientific discourse – if that description be granted, as I think it might, to 'depth psychology'. Here is a model whose articulation possibilities in our own day begin to measure up perhaps to those of economy in an earlier day, though the specific brand of discourse is vastly different – as different indeed as the world of feeling and the world of things, as the world of depth psychology and the world of Whittier and Cowper.

But my last point is no less important. Did not Tillich say, and Robinson after him, 'He who knows about depth, knows about God', and 'Depth is what the word God means'?

Here then is a further parallel between the model of 'depth' and the model of economy. For in that earlier day it could just as well have been said that he who knows economy knows God, and 'economy' is what the word God means.

I have argued then that in the early church 'economy' was one of their most fertile models; that its articulation possibilities were enormous: it combines the broad theme of an over-all providence, what is traditionally called 'general providence', including what Joseph Butler would have called the moral government of the world, with the theme of a God who is watchful over all our particular needs, a particular providence. Few models could be more prolific in their articulation possibilities. We saw how the model of economy could enable us both to speak of the mysteries of a general providence and also to talk of the intimacy of a personal encountering.

We then turned to the second feature which is characteristic of a model. We saw how easily discourse deriving from the model of economy can, in principle, touch down on the world around us to be giving, where it can, 'empirical fit'. But this led us to discuss some of the hazards surrounding a doctrine of both general and particular providence.

I then concluded by drawing a parallel between the model of economy and the case in our own day of the model of depth. As some might say today: 'He who knows about depth, knows about God', and 'Depth is what the word God means', so in an earlier date, it might have been said: 'He who knows economy knows God', and 'economy' is what the word God means. Perhaps the new model, like the old, points to a theological perspective which unites flexibility and mystery, and is seriously concerned with a secular apologetic.

NOTES

1. Op. cit., S.P.C.K. 1952, p. 57.
2. Op. cit., p. 59.
3. Op. cit., p. 65.
4. Ibid.
5. Op. cit., p. 66.
6. Op. cit., p. 63.
7. Op. cit., Methuen ⁵1933, p. 40.
8. Op. cit., p. 39.

III

The Model of Presence

We now come to our third attempt to trace logical pathways through theological discourse, and in this lecture it will be the model of 'presence' which occupies our attention. Unlike the model of 'economy', here is a word – 'presence' – that is constantly on our lips. Prayer, it has often been said, is the practice of the presence of God; books of prayer are titled *Into His Presence*; and it has been rightly pointed out that genuine religion and a sense of God's presence are invariably found together: 'A living sense which passes beyond the evidence of the senses'. But what sort of 'nearness' is this? How is God present? How do we pass beyond the evidence of the senses? What is the point of the metaphors 'awakening of the mind', 'bring home' something to ourselves? What logical patterns can we discern in talk about the presence of God? How can we unravel this area of discourse? Unravelling is certainly needed. So what I propose to do is first to say something about the presence of God, and to elucidate this phrase in terms of my own empirical approach to theological phrases, and then to conclude with a remark on idolatry and some implications for prayer. Even to speak of the presence of God is to raise a logical problem at the outset. Let me put the problem like this.

On the one hand there is the tradition that 'the most High dwelleth not in houses made with hands' (Acts 7.48, Stephen's speech), and with this we may compare Solomon's prayer (I Kings 8.27), 'Heaven and the heaven of heavens cannot contain thee; how much less this house which I have builded?' Again of Solomon (II Chron. 2.6), 'Who is able to build (God) a house?', and Acts 17.24, 'God that made the world and all things therein, he being Lord of heaven and earth dwelleth not in temples made of hands'. Here is being stressed what is commonly called God's 'ubiquity', 'omnipresence', according to which God is not locatable; God is everywhere.

Yet on the other hand, there is discourse which speaks of God here and now, which speaks of God as present in this place or that. Here is God locatable. Compare Gen. 28.16, Jacob's dream: 'Surely the Lord is in this place and I knew it not . . . this is none other but the house of God, and this is the gate of heaven': the Lord in this place.

Put the problem like this. How can God be talked of as both locatable and not locatable? How can we construe language which talks of God 'here and there' – yet 'everywhere'? Is part of our difficulty the fact that we tend to trade in spatial images and to think them descriptive? Perhaps. Is the answer that we become aware of God 'here' or 'there': but that God is present 'everywhere'? But does that quite meet the difficulty? What, then, is the empirical basis for this assertion: that God is present everywhere? What is the empirical anchorage of God's ubiquity?

God's ubiquity/omnipresence is sometimes spoken of as God's 'ordinary presence', and as Father Aelred Graham says in his book, *The Love of God*:

This presence, it may be noted, is but a logical consequence of the act of creation. . . [God] must be intimately present to all His creatures. We speak of God being present in this way 'by His power' or 'through virtual contact'; since, however, the divine power is in reality identical with God Himself it follows that He is present by His very substance in all things. Further, this presence is not limited to the instant of creation; it must last as long as God preserves His creatures in being, for this conservation is nothing less than the continuance of the creative act. Just as the sun must shine as long as the object it enlightens is to remain illuminated, so God must continue to give each of His creatures its existence without which it cannot continue to be.[1]

Again:

God is in all things by His essence, power and presence, according to His one common mode of being present, namely, as the cause existing in the effects which participate in His goodness (i.e. by His ubiquity). Above and beyond this common mode, however, there is one special mode belonging to the rational nature wherein God is said to be present as the object known is in the knower, and the beloved in the lover – *sicut cogitum in cognoscente, et amatum in amante.* And since the rational creature, by its operation of knowledge and love, reaches to God Himself, according to this special mode God is said not only to exist in the rational creature, but also to dwell therein as in His own temple. So no other effect can be put down as the reason why the divine person is in the rational creature in a new mode, excepting sanctifying grace. Accordingly only as a result of sanctifying grace is a divine person sent and does He proceed in the order of time. Likewise we are said to possess only what we can freely use or enjoy: and to have the power of enjoying the divine person can only be according to sanctifying grace. And yet the Holy Spirit is possessed by man, and dwells within him, in the very gift of sanctifying grace. Hence the Holy Spirit Himself is given and sent.[2]

Here is God as 'the immanent cause'.[3] But where is the empirical anchorage for such assertions? Graham answers: It is rather a matter of getting us to 'see'; to 'see' beyond the evidence of our senses.[4] So to understand 'omnipresence' or 'ubiquity' we take as our starting point things, 'the evidence of our senses'. We become aware of God's presence when in some way it is disclosed to us through and beyond them, i.e. when in a survey of such events a disclosure occurs in relation to which we are relatively passive: and if we speak of 'God' as the active agent in all things, we are calling what discloses itself there 'God'. Ubiquity, in other words, points to the otherness which any and every cosmic disclosure reveals. Ubiquity is not a model; it is a word meant to recall a feature of the cosmic disclosure. This I take it to be the truth behind a passage in Aelred Graham:

> The divine ubiquity has nothing to do with space and quantity, as some have thought. It is a gross error to imagine the infinity of God, Who is Being itself, as implying a body without limitations, as though He were like a circle with its circumference everywhere and its centre nowhere. Since He is pure spirit He is above all considerations of space. Though God, by His creative and preservative power, holds all things in existence and is therefore in contact with them, the divine ubiquity is perhaps better conveyed to the mind by the way the voice of a singer is present to those who hear it or the mind to the thoughts which proceed from it than by geometrical imagery. 'God is in all things; not, indeed, as part of their essence, nor as an accident; but as an agent is present to that upon which it works.'[5]

We may now put the initial problem like this. How can God be talked of as both locatable and non-locatable? How can we construe language which talks of God 'here' and 'there' and yet 'everywhere'? There are two answers which we might be tempted to give immediately:

1. Some might say that because God is present everywhere he must *a fortiori* be present here. But that commands the question: Why? Is God present here in the same sense as he is present everywhere? Can the infinite God be finitely present?

2. Some might say that the answer to this question is that God is 'in reality' present 'everywhere' – it is just that we become aware of God 'here' and 'there'. But what do we mean by God 'in reality' being present everywhere?

The difficulty has its logical parallels – and I think they are significant parallels – outside theology. For instance, we can certainly speak of a desk being in this room, of Chicago being located by the side of Lake Michigan. But we cannot speak of the whole universe – that which includes everything – being located anywhere. Again, a point may symbolize a position in space, but space itself cannot be given a position, and needs rather to be talked of in terms of 'infinities' of points. In other words, something of the same problem arises in the case of God's locatable presence on the one hand and God's ubiquity and omnipresence on the other, as in the case of locating some feature of the universe and the whole universe of which it is a part; or in the case of locating a point and the infinite space or spaces of which the point is a part. But encouraging as parallels may be, we do not solve our problem merely by finding echoes elsewhere; indeed, our talk about God's presence may seem to the outsider only a confusion enclosing a vacuity, for in the theological cases in contrast to the mathematical ones, it might be said, nothing seems to have been done by way of logical sorting.

Now I am bold to think that my theory of models and disclosures can help us a little with this problem of how to speak of God as both locatable and non-locatable. Let us, first, go to a typical theological discussion of God's ubiquity or omnipresence such as we find in Father Aelred Graham's book *The Love of God* to which I have already referred. Let us go there for our specimen theological discourse whose logical structure we hope to display. You will recall that Graham suggests – and I think rightly, as you will see presently – that to understand God's omnipresence in principle it is a matter of getting us to 'see', to 'see' what is beyond the evidence of our senses: 'To bring home to ourselves the reality of the divine presence we must pass beyond the evidence of the senses.' So to understand ubiquity or omnipresence we take as our starting point this 'evidence of our senses', and we become aware of God's presence when, in some way or other, it is 'brought home' to us – I say: disclosed to us in and through this evidence. The question then is: in what way?

Let us turn again to Aelred Graham: he remarks that God's ubiquity is sometimes spoken of as God's 'ordinary presence', and he continues:

> This presence, it may be noted, is but a logical consequence of the act of creation. [God] must be intimately present to all His creatures. We speak of God being present in this way 'by His power' or 'through virtual contact'; since, however, the divine power is in reality identical with God Himself it follows that He is present by His very substance in all things. Further, this presence is not limited to the instant of creation; it must last as long as God preserves His creatures in being, for this conservation is nothing less than the continuance of the creative act. Just as the sun must shine as long as the object it enlightens is to remain illuminated, so God must continue to give each of His creatures its existence without which it cannot continue to be.[6]

Again, quoting from St Thomas he remarks:

> God is in all things by His essence, power and presence, according to His one common mode of being present, namely, *as the cause existing in the effects* which participate in His goodness (i.e. present by His ubiquity).[7]

So for Graham, as for St Thomas, ubiquity is grounded in the cosmic disclosure of active power bearing on ourselves, which is generated, for instance, by causal stories. This is the case where a story might begin from the pebbles on a beach whose existence and position was made the subject of a question, and then the basis of a causal explanation constructing a causal array from which in principle nothing was excluded – which would always include terms beyond any that could be specified. As we engage in this exercise and construct an ever-expanding causal array, there might at some point occur a disclosure of an activity bearing on our own, as with a progressively developing pattern we may see at some point what it is meant to represent. In a particular exercise, for example, we might draw a straight line, make a few twists and turns – and someone might suddenly jump to it: we may 'get the message' and say 'The State of Illinois'. But, you may say, how is it that what is disclosed in this way by causal stories, and thus contextualized in those terms, can be said to be identical with what is disclosed in any other stories, and in particular by those which I will mention in a moment and which you might think were more apt to this topic, viz., stories about things that are *present* rather than about *causal* features of the universe? How do *causal* stories help us to elucidate God's *presence*? The answer is, I think, that the two routes *do* lead to the same end in so far as both these routes lead to a cosmic disclosure whose individuation, objectively speaking, is that of the *one* universe itself and which is characterized subjectively and objectively by confronting activities – God's activity meeting our own, God's initiating activity meeting our responsive activity. Indeed, that is only saying from another direction what St Thomas says of God, namely, that for God essence and volition are identical. I quote again from St Thomas:

> God is in all things by His essence, power and presence, according to His one common mode of being present, namely, as the cause existing in the effects which participate in His goodness (i.e. by His ubiquity).

So 'first cause' and 'ubiquity' point to the same disclosure situation as their common ground. But this is to make it very clear that like first cause, ubiquity is no model, but rather a logical kinsman of 'God' himself, pointing to what the disclosure discloses. It is not surprising then that a synonym for ubiquity, i.e. 'omnipresence', is clearly what I call elsewhere a qualified model, where the model is 'present' or 'presence' and the qualifier is the prefix 'omni'. Following what I say about qualified models, if we wish to reach the empirical anchorage of the concept of 'omnipresence', if we want to know what is meant by God's ubiquity, we analyse the word into model and qualifier, *presence* and *omni*, and begin with what we can readily understand, i.e. – present existents – what is with me in the specious present, in order to discover what it is that omnipresence talks about.

We begin then with the model, we begin by asking, What is present to me? What are we now in the presence of? Suppose it is a sunny day: we are more aware of the sun than anything else (or whatever it is that is there in the sky before we begin to infer a 'sun' from the light we now receive), but there is also present the sky, the country, the city, a room, people . . . and so once again we construct a pattern as we try (this time) to survey all that is 'present' as we develop our model in a way in which the qualifier 'omni' would suggest. Now there is no limit to this pattern. As we

seek to include everything that is present to me, so we are
directed to that which is closer and closer, to that which is
'nearer than hands and feet' and even 'closer than breathing' –
until a disclosure of God occurs, there is an 'awakening' of us by
an inward route to reveal something other than myself in
'depth'. If we speak of this as God, then God is a 'ubiquitous',
'omnipresent' God. This is the way in which, as Graham remarks, we 'bring home to ourselves the reality of the divine
presence', and he has said a little earlier, you recall, of what he
calls God's 'nearness', that for the saints it 'is more real for them
than the air they breathe and the material world which surrounds
them'. But this 'divine *presence*', let us notice, must be translated
as 'God's ubiquity': it refers to the active power of God, what
becomes evident to us in any and every cosmic disclosure.

Returning now to our original problem, we note that the word
'presence' is used in two very different, even if related, contexts.
First, as we have seen, it is used for that all-embracing activity
which is revealed in the cosmic disclosure, when 'presence'
should at least have a capital 'P', or alternatively be called omnipresence or ubiquity, whose logical kinsmen are space or the
universe (both these concepts having, on my view, to be grounded
in what occurs respectively, what is disclosed respectively, when
a pattern of points or objects is developed without limit).
Secondly, the word 'presence' is used when and because this
activity is associated with, and particularized in, various terms –
each of which is then, in principle, a model – so that we speak of
God being 'present' as this model is present. Or, alternatively
phrased, *we model God's ubiquity in terms of God's locatable
presence.*

We can now, I hope, see how misleading it is to speak of the
'presence' of God in *both* cases as if they were logical kinsmen.
For 'ubiquity' refers to that infinite, total activity which is given
as the objective reference of every cosmic disclosure reached by
pursuing presence models; whereas to speak of the locatable
presence of God is to speak of that activity of God which is displayed through, and so modelled in terms of, the presence of
finite things and persons.

With this much logical sorting I think we can better understand what is often said about God's locatable presence, and we
can do this without in any way making God one of ourselves or

involving ourselves in those location difficulties which so much tantalize Bishop John Robinson, not least when a scientific universe seems to leave no house-room for God. For all *location* of God, so phrased, is in fact only a *compact* way – and if taken at nothing more than its face value, and if restricted to its face value, a very misleading way – of *modelling God's ubiquity*, that confronting activity disclosed in a cosmic disclosure; only a compact way of modelling God's ubiquity in terms of the presence of this or that particular object.

Let me take a number of particular examples. It might have been thought antecedently that God would never be located as a physical object. But recall 'the pillar of cloud by day, and the pillar of fire by night' of Ex. 13.21f. Does this make God present precisely as the cloud is present, and in that way locatable? No. My reason for saying this is as follows. If you look at A. H. McNeile's Westminster Commentary on *Exodus*, you will find him remarking that, 'It is not impossible that the traditions of a guiding cloud may have had a natural basis.' Indeed, I hope it is not – for without that natural basis I would see no hope of avoiding a theology at one and the same time irrelevant and logically hazardous. McNeile then continues:

The custom is frequently noted in early times of carrying braziers containing burning wood at the head of an army or caravan, and the fire indicated, by night, the line of the march. Curtius relates it of Alexander's march through Babylonia (v.ii.7), and of the Persians generally (III.iii.9). In modern times travellers speak of it in Arabian caravans, and in Palestine. See Harmer, *Observations* ii.278; Frazer, *Golden Bough* (2), i.305. But, as so often, a natural custom or phenomenon rises, in the Hebrew tradition, to a beautiful and spiritual conception, in which all thought of the origin is lost.[8]

Here was a fire or a cloud locating a community; this was a model which, when some spectacular cloud or fire disclosed God (and perhaps that occasion was an eruption of Mount Sinai which I mentioned in the previous lecture), enabled the Hebrews to talk of God's presence here in terms of this fire and cloud leading and guiding them. God did not exist as a cloud or fire existed, but his ubiquity, 'presence', 'objectivity', was mediated, modelled in a particular event. Here was an event in which a cosmic activity was pin-pointed; here was a finite projection of a cosmic ubiquity.

But if God is associated with finite groups of events enabling us to speak of the 'presence' of God, what better than the personal model? He has a wonderful 'presence', we say of some outstanding character. So it is that when Christians have spoken of God as localized in certain events or, as I would prefer to say, in terms of a finite model, this model has often been that of personal presence.

Let me next turn to another quotation from Graham, which quotation includes another from St Thomas:

> What distinguishes God's presence in the soul by grace from His ordinary presence by ubiquity is the fact that He exists therein, no longer simply as an immanent cause, but 'as the object known is in the knower and the beloved in the lover'.[9]

But when the presence of the beloved in the lover models and interprets the ubiquity of God as it can be expressed through a locatable presence; when the activity of the lover is a response to the initiative of God arising around the beloved in a cosmic disclosure, we are reminded how close the model of personal, loving presence comes to the model of Spirit, for we have here 'indwelling' which is interpreted in the doctrine of the Spirit in terms of activities in mutual accord, interpreted now in terms of intimacy of presence, nearness of being. It is interesting that very soon in the same passage St Thomas begins to talk of the indwelling God, and of the indwelling Holy Spirit: 'God is present as the object known is in the knower, the beloved in the lover', when the Holy Spirit 'dwells within' man. Which means that we have another example of our point that every cosmic disclosure can be spoken of in terms of God's presence; and we may recall that in the Old Testament the *ruach*, 'Holy Spirit', Haggades and the Shekinah ('the cloud of God's presence') were sometimes equated and used interchangeably. We also have another example of that interweaving of discourse from different models which gives theology both its rich and its logically complex character.

Let me now broaden our reflections in the direction of the two topics of idolatry and prayer respectively. Let us first see how on this view idolatry could arise.

We shall certainly be idolatrous if we take God's presence to be the presence of a fire or a cloud, or a person, the presence of some locatable human being or state of affairs. The error here is twofold – or two versions of the same error. First: it gives the models

the status and existence of God, and second: it does this when,
and because, it disastrously takes the model as a substitute
picture for God. But idolatry can be avoided and we can legiti-
mately speak of God's presence in terms of discourse relating to
the presence of fires and persons, if these fires and persons have
the status of models set within and finding their fulfilment in
cosmic disclosures, disclosing God's omnipresence, God's ubiquity, models which are then in this way disclosure models, not
picturing models – still less substitutable pictures of God. Only
people like the Hebrews, filled with a sense of God's ubiquity,
could speak of God walking in the garden in the cool of the day
and escape a crude anthropomorphism. Which in some ways is to
account for the fact that of all theological discourse, that of
prayer, where, for the most part, God's omnipresence is focussed
on the model of a person, seems to the outsider a most pointless
and scandalizing exercise.

So I come to my second topic: Prayer.

Prayer, as I have noted, has been traditionally called 'the
practising of the presence of God'. What implication does my
logical sorting of talk about God's presence have for the practice
of prayer?

1. Since prayer is the practising of God's presence, and since
presence is always a model originating in or pointing to a fulfilment in a cosmic disclosure, the origin or end of all prayer will be
such a cosmic disclosure. The words of a prayer should provide
us with a pathway into God's presence, even though the last
stage of the journey may be made in silence. The words of
prayers should be verbal pathways to a disclosure of God,
evoking an awareness of his activity meeting our own. The words
of a prayer should provide us with reflections appropriate to our
being in God's presence. The words should specify that situation, or describe the circumstances which we offer to God in the
hope that God's saving activity will be disclosed and revealed
through them.

2. Prayer will thus be discourse pointing towards the disclosure at which it aims, or alternatively it will be discourse
appropriate to the cosmic disclosure which has, in one way or
another, already occurred. One way or another it will build on
and be expressed in terms of impersonal and personal models. In
this way we may divide logically the five traditional modes of

prayer – adoration, penitence, intercession, thanksgiving, dedi-
cation – into two groups by seeing them as five different character-
izations of cosmic disclosures which arise around models of
presence. In this way, it would seem that adoration on the whole
characterizes cosmic disclosures occurring around impersonal
models of presence, though prayer of adoration may be discourse
where models – impersonal or personal – are deliberately
jumbled, to limit articulation so as to make more emphatic and
clear what we are trying to articulate – the fact exceeds our
language – and all this so as to lose us in wonder, love, praise,
awe. Penitence presupposes either an impersonal model of
presence like the Moral Law (a mark we have missed), or a
personal model (a will we have spurned). Intercession and
thanksgiving certainly presuppose a personal model, and their
language can never diverge from such a model without being
philosophically scandalous and religiously blasphemous. Dedica-
tion is the active response we make to the activity, God's activity,
which the cosmic disclosure reveals, and it could be a speech-
act-prayer or a behaviour response: a dedicated life. This is why
prayer is continuous with the offering of a life.

3. Perhaps we can see what are the ingredients of a good
prayer, especially a prayer to be shared by people corporately and
often repeated, such as a collect:

(a) Its introductory language must lead us into God's pre-
sense and be logically suited to and adequate for that task. This
means in particular that the personal words it contains will be
suitably qualified.

(b) The phrases of the prayer must be consistent with our
doctrine of God, and for the Christian this will relate in particular to doctrines of God's love and grace. Further, this condition
would exclude prayers couched in impersonal terms, or prayers
whose language is modelled on the slot machine or manipulation
techniques. It would also exclude certain understandings of the
'pressure model' which supposes a thousand prayers, simply by
being said and repeated, to be a thousand times more effective
than one. Further, the personal words providing us with a pathway into God's presence must be such as to license the discourse
that follows in the body of the prayers.

(c) The prayer must name a situation or some state of affairs
which can, in principle, be a focus of God's activity, whether as

directed to ourselves, or influencing in some way the circumstances we have named, or both.

We started with a difficult problem which talk of God's presence inevitably raises. How can God be both locatable and non-locatable; here in this place, and yet such that the heaven of heavens cannot contain him? What I have offered you by way of a solution to this problem of theological discourse is the suggestion that what is sometimes called God's 'ordinary presence', non-locatable presence, is better – and less misleadingly – called God's ubiquity or omnipresence. Such ubiquity is revealed in each and every cosmic disclosure: it relates to that activity, power, other than ourselves, which any and every cosmic disclosure discloses.

It is this ubiquity that we then model in terms of God's locatable presence; and such a locatable presence can be that of an impersonal cloud or a personal love.

With that background we saw in what idolatry fundamentally consists: it consists in giving a model the status of God. Another view of this error is to say that it confounds picture-models, i.e. models which are miniatures of what they represent, and disclosure models, which are models licensing more or less adequate discourse about what has been disclosed: talk about what inspires, root of Jesse, mystic rose, stem, babe of Bethlehem. Finally, I showed what emerged as the principles of prayer – and had a word on the practice of prayer when this 'practising of the presence of God' is set against the background of our earlier discussion.

NOTES

1. Aelred Graham, *The Love of God*, Fontana Books 1964, p. 236.
2. Op. cit., p. 240.
3. Op. cit., p. 241.
4. Op. cit., p. 234.
5. Op. cit., p. 236.
6. Op. cit., p. 237.
7. Ibid.
8. A. H. McNeile, *Exodus*, Hodder and Stoughton 1917, p. 82.
9. Graham, op. cit., p. 241.

IV

The Use of these Models in Christian Discourse

In this fourth lecture I would like to take further the implication for Christian discourse of what we have said earlier about the models of spirit, economy and presence. As a preliminary to this let me say what interpretation I would give to the general basis of the Christian faith.

Plainly, the Christian religion takes its rise from Jesus of Nazareth. It originates in the challenge he made on men – a challenge which the gospel writers tried to present and to portray in their narratives – a challenge which on my view was grounded in a cosmic disclosure, and being so grounded naturally led to Christians being articulate about Jesus in terms of God. There was discerned in Jesus that same individuation which was disclosed in and through the universe. In other words, it was as and when a cosmic disclosure occurred around him – and we need not now settle as to whether it often occurred in his lifetime or whether it occurred more often when men looked back on his life viewed in the full perspective of the resurrection and its sequel. Whenever it occurred, it was as and when such a cosmic disclosure occurred around him that men spoke and have spoken of the activity of God.

In the light of our previous discussion and against the broad interpretation of the Christian faith which I have just sketched, what more natural than that this activity of God in Jesus Christ, this activity of God which is the gospel, the 'good news', should be talked of in terms of spirit, economy and presence. I propose to say something about each in turn.

Specifically Christian discourse about the Holy Spirit

Our expectations are fulfilled when, early in the gospels, and not unexpectedly in St Luke's gospel, we have this activity of God in Christ spoken of in terms of the Spirit. Recall that in his conception the power of the Most High overshadowing – God's activity – is spoken of as the coming of the Holy Spirit: Gabriel's message: 'The Holy Spirit will come upon you and the power of the Most High will overshadow you' (Luke 1.35). It is hardly surprising that we find that in some manuscripts the phrase 'Holy Spirit' is here interchangeable with 'God'. For what is being talked about, if our earlier discussion is correct, is that initiating activity of God, for which a movement of air – breath or wind – supplies a model, an initiative of God which is known in the cosmic disclosure in which such a model is set.

For the second example, take the baptism of Jesus: again the activity of God spoken of in terms of the Spirit: 'The Holy Spirit descended on Jesus in bodily form as a dove' (Luke 3.22). Here, incidentally, is another example of a feature of theological discourse we have had cause to notice already, the matching and interlocking of models for God's activity. We might even think that in this case the movement of air was the physical feature which supplied the link between Spirit discourse on the one side, the flight of a dove on the other. In any event, we had examples earlier, you recall, of fire and spirit, oil and spirit, water and spirit. But I do not mention it because it is just another example. It is more. For now I would like to suggest that Christian discourse is particularly distinctive in having an unprecedented interlocking of Spirit and other models in its endeavour to talk of God's activity in Christ. On the whole, though I did not even hint at this earlier, it is only rarely that in the Old Testament we find the model of Spirit associated with other models for God's activity such as fire or oil or rain. Indeed, let me confess that I had no small difficulty in choosing the examples I did choose in my first lecture precisely on this account. But when we come to the New Testament the matter is altogether different; models for God's activity are paired up very frequently indeed. We have already had our first example: the flight of a dove and spirit. Others will occur at once to you: 1. James was baptized, said John, with the Holy Spirit and with fire; 2. the passage from Isa.

58 linking the Spirit and anointing is explicitly given in the sermon at Nazareth (Mark 6.1–6 par); 3. John 4.5 speaks of those who are to be born of water and the Spirit; 4. in Acts 2.2 there was the rush of a mighty wind, there appeared tongues as of fire . . . and all were filled with the Holy Spirit. And the reason for this interlocking being a far more common factor in the New Testament than in the Old Testament? My suggestion is that only in this way could the writers make a specifically Christian claim, viz., that this was, by contrast with earlier understandings of God's activity, a special activity – one which was unique so that it could not be talked about in terms of the single models which hithertofore had largely sufficed. Here was something – the activity of God in Christ – which demanded a rich piling up of models. Notice we have always to do this sort of piling up when we want to claim something as unique. Recall indeed the old popular song: You're the salt in my porridge, sugar in my tea, cream in my coffee – all meant to express that which was by its very uniqueness defying expression. The implication is that if we want the so-called secular world to understand the interlocking of models which (on this view) express the distinctive claim of the Christian faith, we have to start by pointing to the pile-up of models even in a popular song. I might further add that a possible implication of this interlocking of models in Christian discourse is that there was also a double sense of mystery; while men, in terms of a double model, could now say more about God – could articulate the gospel – they were all the more conscious of leaving a double portion unsaid. The pairing of models then can be regarded as a logical feature by means of which to express the Christian claim for a particular unique activity of God in Christ. Now another point. With activity so often modelled in terms of a Spirit, it is not surprising that the activity of God in Christ is spoken of as the 'Spirit of Christ' and that 'the Spirit of God' and 'Christ' are often interchangeable when the context is unambiguous, e.g. Rom. 8.9, 11. You are in the Spirit if the Spirit of God really dwells in you. Anyone who does not have the Spirit of Christ does not belong to him. But if Christ is in you, if the Spirit of him who raised Jesus from the dead dwells in you, he will give life to your mortal bodies. Let me paraphrase it: You display distinctive Christian activity if this is a response to the activity of God meeting you intimately. Who does not live as

responding actively to the activity of God in Christ does not belong to him. But if you live with the activity of God in Christ bearing intimately on you – if the activity of God which can be seen in the resurrection bears intimately on you – he will . . .

These are the kind of pathways I have been tracing for you through discourse about the Spirit. So far the matter may seem very straightforward, though I may perhaps claim that the possibility of this kind of paraphrase points to the reliability of my logical proposals, and may encourage you to trace for yourselves some similar paths through theological discourse.

But I will now pass to some difficulties. First, there have been those who have supposed the word 'Spirit' somehow to name or describe a feature of God; who have given this enhanced logical status to 'Spirit' – or rather have tried to pay the Spirit an empty, a bogus, logical compliment – and, necessarily, at the cost of blinding themselves to the true status and significance of other models like fire and water which are not mere metaphors or visual aids for teaching. As representative of this mistake, I mention one who came nearer than others to discerning the logic of the matter and whose book – popular about forty years ago not least in the USA – has the significant title *Emblems of the Holy Spirit*. So I mention F. E. Marsh not at all because he, more than anyone else, mistook the status of words like spirit and fire and water in Christian discourse, but rather because while making that mistake he came, I think, closest to success of all the many who have spoken and will speak like him – closest to recognizing the logical paths which could be traced through the theological discourse used in preaching.

Because of the association of Spirit with dove, and with water and fire and oil, he claims that this makes possible talk of the Spirit in phrases like the following. Even restricting ourselves to the Bible for discourse about doves, the Spirit, i.e. God's activity, can now be spoken of in a dove context as gentle in manner (Matt. 10.16); constant in love (S. of Sol. 5.12); as swift of wing, beautiful in its plumage, social in its habits, discriminating in food (as contrasted with the ravens). So the Spirit is associated with gentleness, beauty, love, constancy, discrimination, fellowship, swift service. Because of its link with discourse about *water*, the Spirit can be said to cleanse and purify, produce growth and revive; because of its links with discourse about *fire*, the Spirit can be said to purify, penetrate, soften and harden, warm, cheer, test, illuminate; because of its links with discourse about *oil*, the Spirit can be said to illuminate and to heal.

Now of course I am not complaining about or in any way questioning the vast areas of articulation that these different models make possible: indeed, I think that logically Marsh's book is a most significant exercise in the articulation possibilities of models and in the interweaving of discourse from different models. The only mistake, as I see it, is that it is God's activity – not the Spirit of God – which can be expressed in these terms; for the Spirit is a model as much as dove or water or fire. So his book should rather be titled: not *Emblems of the Holy Spirit*, but *Emblems of God's Activity*.

The second difficulty is more serious and far-reaching, and arises because there was another model altogether which was used to be articulate about God's activity in Christ, viz., a father sending his son. Into the origins of this model we need not enquire; whether it was suggested by the very phrases used by Jesus himself, whether it was suggested by the parable of the wicked husbandmen, are questions which we need not go on to discuss here. But it cannot be disputed that here was an influential model which originated, one way or another, in a cosmic disclosure whose focus was Jesus of Nazareth. Whether as the speaker of a parable which was isomorphous with many of the events of his own life, or as the user of the phrase in circumstances where men were aware of the whole universe coming alive around him; here was a model born in a cosmic disclosure and making possible discourse about the significance of Jesus.

Let me see if we can clear at least one pathway through discourse about the Spirit by doing something to sort out the relations between these two models, the model of Spirit and the model of a Father sending his Son.

My suggestion will be that as a consequence of coming alongside this other influential model, the model of Spirit was contextualized in two very different ways. It continued to be used as what might be called a 'dominant model' – a model which talks of the activity of God – indeed of the activity which is God; and here I may remind you of St Thomas's assertion that the essence of God and his volition are the same. There is the sense of Spirit with which hitherto we have been largely concerned.

But the model of Spirit was now also used in a more restricted manner, to speak about this activity which is God, directed to, discernible in, Jesus of Nazareth or later directed to, discernible in the church. This was a particularized community with, or characterized by, a particularized structure, its ministry; a particularized book, the Bible; and particularized means, and activities, the sacraments; all expressing a particularized activity of God which was continuous with God's activity in Christ. Here was the Holy Spirit as the 'Paraclete' which continued Christ's work. It is in this second case then that we have a narrower sense of 'Holy Spirit' in so far as it was associated first with Jesus and then with the Christian community, its life and its members, and undoubtedly this is the general New Testament sense.

Now to the difficulty which arises when the restricted model of Holy Spirit is associated with the alternative model of 'Father and Son'. When this association occurs, 'Holy Spirit' is a model which is assimilated to and takes its place alongside 'the Son', and in this setting the task of theologians is to elaborate rules by which talk of the one is to be related to talk of the other.

For this purpose, i.e. for expressing logical rules to guide discourse, the Fathers devised many pictures which acted as mnemonics to help us to be more reliably articulate in terms of these two models for God's particularized activity: Holy Spirit and Father sending the Son.

One such picture was afforded by the concept of *hyparxis*, of which considerable use was made by Irenaeus. This afforded a picture of coming forth, and three ways of coming forth were distinguished, each having its distinctive label: unbegotten, begotten, proceeding. These words thus became mnemonics, reminder slogans, for the better ordering of Christian discourse; mnemonics, not descriptions of some heavenly going on, which could be discerned through the long-range theological telescope! Here were mnemonics for reminding those who supplemented the model of Father sending Son with the model of Holy Spirit that:

1. Discourse derived from the constituent element Father was logically prior to discourse from other constituent characters. Father represented an ultimate presupposition. Here is the point of 'unbegotten'.

2. The phrase 'the Son' cannot occur in ordinary assertions about men without qualification; here is the logical point of 'begotten not made'.

3. Adequate assertions about the Holy Spirit are needed to presuppose assertions about the Father and the Son. This was the logical point of the doctrine of the procession, at least when to this was added the *filioque* clause. No need to go into details now, I simply want to make the point that these highly stylized doctrines are not descriptions of what some have called the inner life of the Godhead; they are rules for our consistent talking, rules for sorting out discourse from models.

An alternative mnemonic for the ordering of Christian discourse can be found in Cyril, who has a picture of interweaving which I see again as a mnemonic reminding us that logically complete talk of God will demand all three strands. Though I am bound to say that a better mnemonic-picture might be the mixing of distinguishable rhythms to give one dance. Certainly, even in the early Fathers – I am thinking of some writings ascribed to Gregory of Nyssa – there was growing up the idea of the words Father, Son and Holy Spirit characterizing three logically different strands of discourse, all of which were needed to talk about God. This idea of logical unity with logical diversity was eventually continued and explicated in the doctrine of *perichōrēsis*. But without going into further details, what I am saying is that the point of all these picturesque stories is a logical one, viz., to remind the reader that in discourse deriving from the model of Father sending Son, and its associated (restricted) model of Holy Spirit, the elements Father, Son and Holy Spirit designate three logically distinct strands of discourse for talking about the activity of God which is the Christian gospel. These strands have further to be united if they are to become logically complete talk of the activity of God which is the gospel.

But let not my main point be lost in detail. Here in these highly stylized doctrines of *hyparxis*, *perichōrēsis* and the rest, are pictures acting as mnemonics – slogan reminders – to suggest various logical rules. They are not, *not*, models, let alone picturing models. They are of a different logical order altogether, for their purpose is to guide our paths in Christian discourse which proceeds from a multitude of models. The grave error, of course, as I have already implied, would be to take these mnemonics, these highly stylized logical stories, as pictures of God; logically it is even a greater blunder than taking models as pictures of God, for we are one stage further removed. If you ask, and naturally, 'But what justification can be given for these logical rules, for these mnemonic pictures?', it is not now, I think, primarily in terms of the empirical fit of the discourse to which they lead, but rather in terms of the coherence and consistency and comprehensiveness and simplicity of the total Christian scheme, and this would presuppose, for the Fathers, a scheme coherent with the discourse to be found in the Scriptures.

What I have said can now be given a wider context (indeed its full context), if we remind ourselves of what we said in earlier lectures and mentioned near the start, about the dominant model of Holy Spirit, or Spirit – the model which expresses God's activity in all its fullness: which expresses the activity which is God.

This indeed makes 'Spirit' the model for discussing what has been traditionally talked of in terms of the model of 'one substance'; and the models of Father, Son and Holy Spirit (in the restricted sense) now designate three logically different articulations for talking of the activity which is God when this activity is particularized in Jesus of Nazareth.

Just two corollaries:

1. *What of Augustine's claim that the Spirit is a bond of union between the Father and the Son?* This I see as logically yet more complex. For it is using Spirit, often contextualized in terms of love which is a fruit of the Spirit, using Spirit now as a mnemonic for logical pathways through Christian discourse. What it cannot (logically cannot) be doing – though much theological discussion sounds as though it thought Augustine was doing this – is to have the Holy Spirit both as a relation and a thing at the same time. On the other hand, we must not be too sure we have understood. Talk of the Spirit as a bond of union might be interpreted quite reasonably in terms of the Spirit's being an alternative model to the 'one substance' which does indeed unite Father and Son. So at least two placings then are possible for Augustine's claim; sometimes alternative logical paths are traceable in theological discourse.

The second corollary:

2. *Is the Holy Spirit a person?* This question is better phrased: Does talk about the Holy Spirit conform to a personal logic?

In so far as the phrase is associated with what is characteristically personal behaviour, it will conform to a personal logic; likewise a giver of gifts will conform to a personal logic. But (as we have seen) discourse about the Spirit originated in situations of gale-force winds or refreshing breezes, so not all talk of the Spirit need have a personal logic. There would seem to be no reason why we should exclude non-personal language from a doctrine of the Spirit, any more than we exclude it from other models of the activity of God. Here, as elsewhere, we shall be wise to be logically flexible in our approach to theology.

The model of 'economy'

These recent reflections of a Trinitarian sort have brought us conveniently close to the specifically Christian use of the model of 'economy'. Because, as we saw, the model of 'economy' allowed for discourse relating to particular groups of events, particular providence, the activity of God could be talked of not only in terms of a general providence, but also in terms of groups of events which in this way were given a special significance. As I said in my second lecture, those who knew God's over-riding providence could also meet God as a friend. Hence it is not surprising to find 'economy' used in a specifically Christian sense, both of the eucharist and of the incarnation. For example, Prestige reminds us that:

> In Epiphanius 'The Economy' is used as a title of the Eucharistic service, just as 'Celebration' or 'The Sacrament' are sometimes employed in English: usually he adds the distinguishing words 'or worship' to the title. Thus (*haer.* 75.3) the bishop and the priest likewise perform the economy of worship; in some places, he says, the worship of economy (reversing the order and dependence of the terms) is performed on the fifth day (*exp. fid.* 22), and they perform memorials for the departed, making prayers and worships and economies (*ib.* 23).[1]

He concludes:

> It need only be added that the supreme instance of divine economy, whether in the sense of dispensation, condescension, or special providence, was exhibited in the Incarnation, for which the word 'oekonomia', without any verbal qualification, is the regular patristic term from the third century onwards.

From the general standpoint it is, I think, significant that this reference to worship is added. For this implies that, as we have suggested, the model of 'economy' ever finds its fulfilment in a cosmic disclosure: that is precisely what worship should be.

But to link this section more explicitly with my earlier Trinitarian remarks, we may recall that in the early church 'economy' came to be used to talk of what is sometimes spoken of as the 'organic unity' of God, and we may take Tertullian as a particular example. Let me quote from Prestige, who reminds us of the significance of Tertullian's contribution. He reminds us of what is, of course, the basis of all Trinitarian doctrine: belief in one God, yet talk of divinities in relation to Jesus and the Holy Spirit:

> The recognition of divine monarchy and the proclamation of a divine triad were originally presented as independent facts, but they were facts which would clearly need a considerable amount of reconciliation in a philosophical mind, so soon as their contrasting truth was firmly held and fairly faced. This Tertullian attempted to achieve.[2]

How did he achieve it? Continuing the comment from Prestige, the point is that:

> Tertullian's conception of divine unity, on the other hand, rests on his doctrine of 'economy', that the unity constitutes the triad out of its own inherent nature, not by any process of sub-division, but by reason of a principle of constructive integration which the godhead essentially possesses. In other words, his idea of unity is not mathematical but philosophical; it is an organic unity, not an abstract, bare point.
>
> When Tertullian employs economy, which he transliterates instead of translating, as a means of expressing the nature of the divine unity, the reference which lies behind this usage is mainly to the sense of interior organisation. The same word had been used in a somewhat similar sense by Quintilian in writing of literary craftsmanship. Quintilian (*inst. or.* 3.3.9) states that Mermagoras puts judgement, division, and arrangement, and whatever belongs to delivery, under the head of economy, which, he says, is a name taken in Greek from the oversight of domestic affairs and is here employed metaphorically; it lacks a Latin equivalent.[3]

But there are two ways of viewing Tertullian's use of the model of economy to elucidate Trinitarian possibilities.

1. It may be no more than an imaginative picture for the unity of God doing no more than showing how it is possible to talk of a 'triad of divine Persons' as 'one'. In this sense 'economy' would be no more than what we have called a 'logical mnemonic'.

2. 'Economy' may have a usefulness in Trinitarian theology

because of the ways in which it models God's activity permitting of three particularizations of activity, three 'deviations'. This may be what Prestige is saying about the broad outline of Tertullian's doctrine:

> He recurs again and again to the same conception of economy. His reference has already been quoted to the simple believers who were startled at the economy for fear of reversion to polytheism, not understanding that although He is the sole God, yet He must be believed in with His own economy. The numerical order and collocation (dispositio) of the triad, Tertullian says (*ib.* 3), was assumed by his opponents to be a division of the unity; whereas the unity, devolving the triad out of its own self, is not destroyed by it, but is 'distributed', or dispensed, or organised, or methodised, or functionally constituted – Tertullian's term is literally untranslatable, but the paraphrases which have been used give some representation of its general sense. The actual words are, 'quando unitas, ex semetipsa derivans trinitatem, non destruatur ab illa sed administretur.' The last word is transparently the equivalent of the Greek 'economise' (*oikonomeō*). It implies, at least in some sense, that the substance of godhead is relayed in turn to each Person of the triad; in so far, the meaning is simply distributive. But, as dispositio expresses not merely distribution but also methodical arrangement, so economy carries a strong implication of constructive order and system. The instances quoted above prove this.
>
> In this quotation, then, the idea of functional organisation is to be emphasised.[4]

Eventually, you will see, Tertullian associates economy with mystery; he is anxious that 'the mystery of the economy is preserved'. Here would be the model of 'economy' elucidating – perhaps we could say making possible – Trinitarian discourse, and suggesting how three particularized activities, significantly distinguishable activities, could be as one. 'Three persons in one substance', and if this account of both persons and substance is thus of activity bringing them closely together, this may be one reason why in the discussion of Christian doctrine the words *substantia, persona, ousia, prosopon, hypostasis* were often used.

But grateful as we may be to see that value in the model of economy, remember 'economy' is still only a model, however far-reaching its use. It would certainly be *fatal* to picture God as a sort of three-term administration. But that is an old story, and I will say no more except to leave you with that question to which I do not know the answer. Why did 'economy', a model with all these possibilities, virtually disappear from theology? I do not know: some might say because Western approach edged out the

Eastern approach which was much more fertile, much more subtle and possessed much more sense of mystery. But at least I have been trying to rehabilitate it!

We must not suppose that theological models, even the best ones, are picturing models.

The model of 'presence'

So now I turn to the model of 'presence' in specifically Christian discourse. I will take only one area, its use in speaking of eucharistic presence. Looking at the matter quite afresh, it is plain that what is needed here is once again, as in the last lecture, to see how, and under what conditions, we can talk of the presence of God in terms of particular elements, like bread and wine, i.e. how we can talk of God's ubiquity in terms of his localizable presence in the eucharistic elements.

This means in effect that doctrines of eucharistic presence ought to be illuminated:

1. By keeping firmly to the distinction between that presence of God which is omnipresence, which is ubiquity, and the models, in this case the bread and wine, by which that presence is talked about.

2. Thereafter by a sorting between the metaphors and models used to talk about this localizable presence. Certainly, eucharistic doctrine needs illuminating.

We may recall here some comments by C. C. Richardson, in a recent article in the *Journal of Theological Studies*:

> Eucharistic doctrine is exceedingly complex, because traditional language can obscure all sorts of ambiguities, and in consequence the most penetrating questions to ask are often disregarded. Moreover, all the unresolved problems of statements about God and propositions in Christology find a focus here. Unless some prior decisions are made on those issues, eucharistic theology wanders in the dark. Until we are sure what we mean by speaking of God's activity in history, in nature and in our personal affairs, and until we know what we are talking about in Christological statements, we cannot formulate meaningful doctrines about the Lord's Supper.
>
> There is also a further difficulty. The basic terms appropriate to eucharistic thought are highly symbolic. We seem to be dealing with a metaphor of a metaphor of a metaphor, or a mystery of a mystery of a mystery. By this I refer to the fact that there are three pregnant but esoteric expressions which are not used literally. We speak of the 'body' of

Christ, certainly not meaning the literal, physical body of the first century A.D. We then proceed to speak of 'eating' it, not thereby intending any actual cannibalism – that so-called 'capernaical' view, so 'gross and so dull', as Cranmer says, in unjustly attributing it to Gardiner. Finally, it is all in some way connected with speaking of bread and wine as the body and blood of Christ. We thus appear to move from one obscurity to another, piling metaphor on metaphor, and with each step becoming more and more confused and unsure of ourselves.

So difficult, indeed, does the analysis of eucharistic doctrines become, when we try to ask fundamental questions about the nature of reality, its substance and accidents (for example), or the character of symbolic actions which are directly related to divine activity, that the historian is prompted to classify doctrines purely from their external effect.[5]

Well, what I have tried to do has been some simple exercises in logical placing. A doctrine of the 'real presence' becomes an endeavour to claim in terms of some model of 'presence', and here the models have been very diverse, that the same particularized activity of God terminates in the bread and wine, as terminated in Christ – body and blood.

May I draw out the implications of Richardson's remarks. They afford something of a background to this analysis that I've been trying to outline for you; and on this background we may perhaps sort out some of the obscurities by seeing what logically different models eucharistic theology has involved.

Sometimes the models have been metaphysical: this was the case of the doctrines of transubstantiation, consubstantiation and so on. Sometimes the models have been psychological: this was the case with a Zwinglian remembrance. Sometimes the models have been empirical: this was the case of the Anglican doctrine which, as with Lancelot Andrewes, has modelled the real presence of Christ in the sacraments on the real presence of Christ in the partaking congregation. I think that Richardson's own suggestion of concentrating on the model of 'body' probably unites the empirical and the metaphysical. What would our own reflections from the previous lecture suggest? We might well think that what we said about models of presence suggests that a highly personal model might provide us with the most acceptable articulation. On this view, the sacraments would be efficacious when they disclosed the love of God in Christ – i.e. justified this personal model (love) of presence – as an understanding of God's ubiquity at this point. Christ would then be said to be present in the sacrament as friend meeting friend in love. It is true that we might well be able to give a doctrine of transubstantiation a new look if interpreted in terms of a model for ubiquity which had that logical status, but the danger would always be that a doctrine of transubstantiation seemed to give an impersonal interpretation of the relation between God and man and might even encourage a super-scientific explanation – it might encourage the worst kind of metaphysics.

For, as you may well by now have suspected, I see the theory of models and disclosures *inter alia* as having the widest possible significance: I see models and disclosures as making possible the rehabilitation of a metaphysics. But this will never be a metaphysics of a super-scientific brand. It will be a metaphysics whose motifs are insight and tentativeness. Likewise, when the theory of models and disclosures makes possible, as I believe it does now, understandings of the Christian faith, they are understandings of the faith which highlight the tentative character of theology and to the grounding of all belief in mystery.

So we may despair with the Anglican divine, John Bramhall (1594–1663), of any all-too-articulate eucharistic theology: we protest against those whose theology tears the seamless coat of Christ into pieces; minces faith into shreds and spins it 'into niceties more subtle than the webs of spiders', because curious wits, says Bramhall, 'cannot content themselves to touch hot coals with tongs but must take them up with their naked fingers . . .'

Let not theology be half-witted when its very life is at stake in our contemporary society, and models and disclosures I offer as a recipe to revitalize it.

So the summary. We have been taking further the implication for Christian discourse of what I've said earlier about the models of spirit, economy and presence.

I first showed how in the New Testament there often occurs the pairing of other models with that of Spirit, and I said that this pairing could be regarded as a logical feature by means of which to express the Christian claim for a particular unique activity of God in Christ. I then argued that those who had supposed the word 'Spirit' somehow to name or describe a feature of God, had necessarily done it at the cost of blinding themselves to the true status and significance of other models like fire and water which are not mere metaphors or visual aids for teaching. The Spirit is a model as much as dove or water or fire.

I then looked at the logical difficulties which arose when Holy Spirit as a distinctive Christian model for God's activity in Christ took its place alongside the other model of 'Father and Son', and I said that the task of theologians is to elaborate rules by which talk of the one is to be related to talk of the other.

For this purpose, i.e. for expressing logical rules to guide discourse, the Fathers devised many pictures which acted as mnemonics to help us to be more reliably articulate in terms of these two models for God's particularized activity: Holy Spirit and Father sending the Son. But I repeat, these highly stylized doctrines of *hyparxis*, *perichōrēsis* and the rest, are pictures acting as mnemonics – slogan reminders – to suggest various logical rules. They are not, *not*, models, let alone picturing models. They are of a different logical order altogether – for their purpose is to guide our paths in Christian discourse which proceeds from a multitude of models. The grave error, of course, as I have already implied, would be to take these mnemonics, these highly stylized logical stories, as pictures of God; logically it is even a greater blunder than taking models as pictures of God, for we are one stage further removed. If you ask, and naturally, 'But what justification can be given for these logical rules, for these mnemonic pictures?', it is not now, I think, primarily in terms of the empirical fit of the discourse to which they lead, but rather in terms of the coherence and consistency and comprehensiveness and simplicity of the total Christian scheme, and this would presuppose, for the Fathers, a scheme coherent with the discourse to be found in the Scriptures. I then looked at Augustine's claim and the question whether the Holy Spirit was a person. There would seem to be no reason why we should exclude non-personal language from a doctrine of the Spirit, any more than we exclude it from other models of the activity of God. Here, as elsewhere, we shall be wise to be logically flexible in our approach to theology.

Looking back at Tertullian's use of economy to elucidate Trinitarian doctrine, I said there are two possibilities. Finally, I showed something of the approach to the doctrine of eucharistic presence which our earlier reflections could make possible – and suggested that perhaps the personal model deserved further attention as a means of elucidating 'real presence'.

I concluded with a passage from John Bramhall, which reminded us how in eucharistic theology it is more than ever important to be tentative in theology if we would not strangle it of its life. But is a tentative theology the same as theological atheism? Are models and disclosures a substitute for God? These are the questions which lie behind our next lecture.

NOTES

1. G. L. Prestige, *God in Patristic Thought*, Heinemann, 1936, p. 66.
2. Op. cit., p. 97.
3. Op. cit., p. 99.
4. Op. cit., p. 102.
5. C. C. Richardson, 'Cranmer and Eucharistic Doctrine', *Journal of Theological Studies*, New Series XVI, October 1965, p. 433.

V

Pathways to Theological Atheism

I have tried in these lectures to trace some logical pathways in theological discourse: discourse about the Spirit; discourse about economy, broadening into discourse about God's great and particular providence; discourse about God's presence; specifically Christian discourse about the Holy Spirit, about Trinitarian doctrine and doctrine of eucharistic presence. Our two guiding themes have been models and disclosures. To use the concept of a model encourages us to look at Christian discourse as a complex interweaving of various strands, each of which derives from a particular model, and, as we saw, some of the most highly stylized Christian doctrines have been the means of supplying logical rules to relate these strands and control the development of this discourse.

Now it is evident, on this view of Christian discourse, that:

1. Theology is no straight descriptive language. In an earlier lecture, for instance, I protested against taking spirit as though it named a ghostly figure, taking the procession or *perichōrēsis* as descriptive of the inner life of God.

2. Theology always pays back into that which calls forth a commitment of which the theology is in part an interpretation. My approach, as you will have noticed, may be thought to be characteristic of much contemporary theology, which seems to have an ever-increasing concern with these images, metaphors and models – call them what you will.

This emphasis on images, metaphors and models raises a crucial problem: how can contemporary theologians be sure that they are talking about God – or about anything at all for that matter? Focussing the question on myself: is a cosmic disclosure anything more, at best, than a rather moving, memorable experience determining some attitude to the world – but something quite 'subjective' with no genuine claim to objective reference? Do I regard the Christian faith as anything more than a particular way of looking at the world – a pilgrimage, a vale of soul-making, a way of self-realization through suffering, rather than a tale told by an idiot? Am I offering a Christian faith which, perhaps, has no God?

To point up the problem, let me consider a criticism of contemporary theology made by one of the most sensitive and fair-minded humanists in Great Britain – my friend, Professor R. W. Hepburn. It occurs in a symposium originally held as broadcast talks, published by the BBC in a small book, *Religion and Humanism*. Hepburn has in mind the current theological concern with images, metaphors and models and he comments:

> I am not saying, outrageously, that metaphors are a disease of religious discourse: only that at some point we need to break out of them and talk 'straight' about God and about his relation to the world, and that we are right to feel uneasy with our theologians if they keep treading round the wheel of images.[1]

Professor Hepburn's challenge, it seems to me, presents us with four tasks, if we are to justify our claim that the Christian faith is not just a way of looking at the world, though of course this is part of the truth and an important reminder of the risk of commitment in all religious belief.

1.   If theological assertions – in particular Christian assertions – are to make a genuine religious claim, their topic cannot be restricted to what is seen: the world as it is around us, the world around which the astronaut flies. In other words, there must be some viable concept of the transcendent, the 'supernatural' – call it what you will, and though we call it 'supernatural' it is to use a word than which none could be more misleading. For the concept of the transcendent, while it must go beyond what is seen, must incorporate what is seen as well. In days past, at any rate, the great trouble with those who seemed to safeguard the transcendence of God, or the 'supernatural', was that they were tempted to buy wonderful transcendence at the exorbitant price of a total failure to relate it convincingly to the world we know.

2.   If Christians claim to go beyond picturesque, inspiring

stories, at least talk about God's activity must be literal and univocal, straightforwardly reliable.

3. Christian assertions must be a clearer objective reference. Somewhere or other they must encourage us to appeal to 'what is the case'. This is the point at issue behind the claim for literal language – for literal, unadorned language is commonly thought to guarantee its reference, to guarantee its object – of which it is a plain description.

4. There must be some way of expressing preferences. It must not be the case that the Christian faith is merely one way of looking at the world and that you might or might not fancy this particular view – just as some like oysters and some don't. There must be criteria for reasonable preference.

In short, we shall only face the challenge of contemporary thought, we shall only answer Professor Hepburn's question, we shall only have made a case for going beyond theological atheism when we have:

1. defended our claim for transcendence;
2. justified talk of God's activity;
3. given an account of the reference of theological discourse;
4. given some criteria for reasonable preference between alternative views of the universe – ways of looking at the world.

Let us face these four points in turn.

1. First, then, the need for transcendence, and it must be a transcendence which does not exclude but rather incorporates 'the facts and features of the world'.

This need for transcendence is what Ninian Smart sees as the crucial issue in conversations with the humanists, and it was because he supposed that my view denied and left no room for the possibility of transcendence that he spoke of me in *Theology* for January 1965 as a virtual atheist – with perhaps not much 'virtual' about it.

Renford Bambrough approaches this question by making an illuminating comparison between some current ways of talking about God and our attitude to the Greek gods. Let us suppose, he says,

that Homer is resurrected, and that we are walking with him by the seashore on a stormy day. As we walk along the cliffs Homer may say to us: 'Poseidon is angry today'. And it would be quite natural for us to answer in the same terms, to say: 'Certainly, Poseidon is very angry today'. We both use the same words 'Poseidon is angry'; and yet it is clear that there is a vast difference between what Homer is doing with these words and what we, with our much greater knowledge of meteorology and ocean-ology, are doing with the same words. One way of describing the difference would be to say that when Homer says that Poseidon is angry he is offering what is meant to be an *explanation* of the lashing of the waves, whereas when we say that Poseidon is angry we are giving no more than a picturesque *description* of the lashing of the waves.[2]

Here would be theology styling a way of looking at the world. Bambrough continues:

The same Greek pantheon and the same Greek theology are often used by modern writers for the same purpose of presenting and describing and commenting on exactly the same elements in the experience that we share with the ancient Greeks. We all have experience of the power of Aphro-dite and of the contrary power of Artemis. We have all witnessed conflicts between the powers of destiny and chance and the feebler powers of human choice. We all have experience of the arbitrariness and capricious-ness of the powers of nature and of human nature. We may not agree with him, but Freud was speaking in a way that we can understand, and in a way that any ancient Greek would have understood, when he said that 'dark, unfeeling and unloving powers control man's destiny'.[3]

Here is the use of Greek theology to talk in a colourful way about the world. Bambrough continues:

Bonhoeffer, Bultmann, Tillich, Braithwaite and the Bishop of Wool-wich have done to traditional Christian words something as radical as we have done to the words of Homer and Sophocles. Have they done the *same* thing? Is their talk of God, like my talk of Poseidon and Athena, so different from what such talk used to be that it would be better, clearer, more honest, to find new words for expressing what is in effect a new belief?[4]

Renford Bambrough does not answer the question, but plainly the answer depends entirely on our attitude to the transcendent reference. If all transcendence is denied, it would be more honest to express in different words what is a vastly different belief. But what is involved when transcendence is asserted? Renford Bam-brough himself answers *this* question by saying:

While the remarks of a theologian must be based on familiar or at least accessible facts and features of the world of our ordinary experience, they must also refer to something over and above the facts and features on which they are based.[5]

So to safeguard God's transcendence we must look for a

situation which incorporates both the facts and features of the world of ordinary experience, and something over and above those facts and features. Where can we find this? It is precisely this which I hold is given in cosmic disclosures. Three points here:

(i) Whenever a cosmic disclosure occurs, whenever the universe comes alive about a point, I respond with a commitment, a self-affirmation, I realize myself in that response. Whenever, for example, we respond to a duty which bears down on us with a categorical, all-demanding claim: 'Here I stand and can no other, come what may', it is then, I would say, that we realize our freedom, we offer ourselves in decisive action, to which first-person language is distinctively appropriate.

(ii) Now this decisive action is transcendent because it is something more than observables. On what grounds do we say that? The answer is that all talk about observables is talk about objects, and subjectivity cannot be talked about in terms of the object, the observables which presuppose it. In other words, all talk about objects demands, logically, at least one subject which cannot be, in this sense, objectified; the observer cannot himself be contained in what he observes. As David Hume said long ago, we ourselves cannot be restricted to observables if justice is going to be done to our subjectivity, our uniqueness, our self-identity. There is a logical need to preserve the subject which all third-person assertions about objects logically demands. Linking points one and two together, our subjectivity is known in a self-disclosure which transcends the observables it includes. This transcendent subjectivity is something of which I am aware in using distinctively first-person utterances, this subjectivity is what the doctrine of performatives presupposes. We affirm our subjectivity in using the word 'I', as we name the ship in saying the word in appropriate circumstances.

(iii) Now I grant that we cannot be sure of objective transcendence in the same way as we can be sure of our own subjective transcendence. But to bemoan that fact is to utter a pseudo-regret like regretting that I am not you, that I cannot know your thoughts as I know my own. It is sufficient to realize that the language we use of ourselves and the language we use of the world around us always develops *pari passu*. We come alive as and when the universe comes alive, challenges us, takes the initiative, as we say. But if, in a cosmic disclosure, subject and object are in this way matched, then God's objectivity is disclosed to us as a correlate of our own self-disclosure and we can reasonably claim that our transcendent objectivity remarks our own. There is a subjective and objective transcendence about every cosmic disclosure. Here then is my reply to the question of the transcendent reference of theological discourse. Whether we are justified in slipping in the word 'God' is something I will return to later, at the end of the lecture. For the moment allow it.

2. Now let us pass to the question of talk about activity. And here is a crucial point of whose significance I have only lately been aware. If we are looking for some concept, some feature of the disclosure which characterizes ourselves and what confronts us equally, which we therefore talk about neither equivocally nor analogically but univocally; if we are looking for some phrase which we can use of what confronts us in the same sense as we can use it of ourselves, we have it in 'activity'. For we only know our own activity in matching it with an activity which confronts us. The two exactly interlock; we meet activity in the same sense that we exert it.

So activity is that of which we can speak – even in relation to God – literally: it is for all our discourse a logical primitive.

3. Which brings us neatly, I hope, to the question of objective reference. For here at one and the same time is justified not only the basis for talk – literally, as it would be said – about activity which the Christian needs above all else (the second point), but also (this third point) the claim to objectivity.

The claim for 'objectivity' – 'objective reference' – is grounded in the sense I have of being confronted, of being acted upon, in the discernment I have of some claim impinging on me. I readily grant that this is a particular sense of objectivity: it is not precisely the 'objectivity' (which people are often moved to deny) which belongs to dream images; it is not even precisely the objectivity (which people only too often take as a paradigm of objectivity) which characterizes physical objects. It is not precisely the objectivity which belongs to other people as the topic of social studies. It is better suggested by the objectivity of what declares itself to us – challenges us in a way that persons sometimes do. To put it otherwise. We reach some facts by selection, picking them out, pointing them out: and, for some purposes, in some contexts, we may even pick out persons. But we reach other facts by their disclosing themselves to us, and these are facts such as the facts of duty and the moral law and persons.

The otherness of God may be disclosed to us through:

dream images (as the writer of St Matthew's Gospel believes);
physical objects (as Berkeley believes);
duty and the moral law (as Kant believes);
persons (when we see God in our friends);

but only when dream images, physical objects, duty, persons, become each the focus of a cosmic disclosure. Further, because of the cosmic character of cosmic disclosures there is no sense in talking of anything more than a single individuation in all the cases any more than in talking of there being one universe.

But supposing it be granted that cosmic disclosures in which I am aware of being acted upon, of something (someone) bearing actively upon me, can on this account claim to give us both the objectivity, and a logical, literal base in activity for the reliable language which we seek; how do we test between those who talk of these cosmic disclosures and their activity in different and incompatible ways, who are articulate about these cosmic disclosures in terms of vastly different models?

4. Here is the problem of verification and the problem of reasonable preferences. Now let me grant that I am conscious of being very close to Hepburn. How do we decide between two articulations from cosmic disclosures, between two areas of multi-model discourse? I answer: we shall reasonably prefer that discourse which (*a*) formally is the most simple, coherent, comprehensive and consistent; (*b*) materially establishes the best empirical fit – and by empirical fit I mean the kind of fit presupposed by hymns like those of the kind we were considering when we discussed the model of spirit, and the model of economy: the hymns of Cowper, Tate and Brady, and Whittier, e.g.

God moves in a mysterious way . . .

The bud may have a bitter taste,
But sweet will be the flower.[6]

Experience will decide
How blest they are, and only they,
Who in his truth confide.

All as God wills, who wisely heeds,
To give or to withhold,
That care and trial seem at last,
Through memory's sunset air,
Like mountain ranges overpast,
In purple distance fair.[7]

Let me elucidate my view by reference to Hepburn. Hepburn sees, I would say, that all of us, believers in God or not, do well to acknowledge the occurrence of situations I have called cosmic disclosures, and that what I have called 'qualifiers', while they are the words which cause us trouble in theological language, are, nevertheless, significant in pointing to the grounding of that language in cosmic disclosures. Says Hepburn:

> It is the little words – 'outside', 'inside', 'beyond' – that cause the logical trouble, when they are applied to the world as a whole. . . But do these words *altogether* fail us? Do they not express a range of haunting and memorable human experience at least better than any other words at our disposal? Perhaps we can be empirical even here. For many people there are times when the world loses its ordinariness and takes on a disturbing, derivative, transfigured look; when awe deepens to numinous awe.[8]

It is far too mystical to say that the words do not altogether fail us. Indeed they do not fail us at all. For these qualifiers are the words which have the logic of an imperative which points us forward from models to cosmic disclosure; that which must be the basis for all theological talking; that which Hepburn characterizes elsewhere as 'wonderment, reverence, love, spiritual openness'.

So far so good. But the problem is: what is disclosed? Our talk about what is disclosed has to proceed by an interweaving of discourse from as many models as possible. Ninian Smart rightly recognizes that Hepburn and other humanists, besides believers, have this same 'notion of a quest towards verification'. As Smart says later in the symposium:

> [Hepburn] certainly does imply, does he not, that there are some experiences and attitudes which we commonly call religious which are open to the humanist; and then the constructive task for the humanist, the sensitive humanist, is that of attempting to give a kind of move towards, at any rate, a unified view of the world which does incorporate these facets of experience.[9]

In this sense, I agree, the sensitive humanist and the theist have a common quest. It does not make everybody believers all round, but it does establish similarities which might not have been suspected between the theist's and the humanist's quest and attitude (something which a theist with any conviction of God's over-all creative providence cannot possibly deny and be consistent). But the differences must not be concealed or ignored. The theist can only be a genuine theist if the personal model is a dominant model for his discourse – the model by which most of his discourse is structured when he starts to talk of the activity which confronts him in a cosmic disclosure. But of course the humanist's discourse may be personally structured, and there are those who would in any event counsel a personalistic attitude to the universe. But the major question will be about the multi-model discourse in each case, which is the more comprehensive and has the better empirical fit.

Further, as the second generalization, we return to our original point of that feature which is essential to any genuine theism: there must be an objective reference; and if we are Christians, some defence of taking 'activity' as a concept around whose use no logical suspicions can be aroused.

Now I return to a problem I promised to attend to in this lecture; it is a problem to which I have presupposed the answer from the start, and it can be put as a question: Why should the name 'God' be given for the objective reference of the disclosure? Would it be better to drop the word 'God' altogether? Even if I have established an objective reference, what right have I to call that reference 'God'? On what grounds could I claim that a cosmic disclosure reveals God? My answer is as follows:

1.   Let me begin by using an illustration I have used elsewhere. Suppose we draw a series of regular polygons with an ever-increasing number of sides, and draw them such that their vertices are equidistant from a fixed point. What will we get? The plain down-to-earth man will say, a lot of polygons, and he is obviously right. But is that the whole story? For my purpose I hope not. At some point or other, I suggest, something else may 'strike' us, something else is disclosed, we may say 'a circle'. But for my present purpose it is important that I do not trade on the fact that we all know circles independently. Suppose we did not. Call what is disclosed 'X', then if we wanted to talk of X, to contextualize X, talk of polygons would be a good approximate, indeed the only reasonable approximate, and the more sides the

better. A purchaser wishing to have an X-like swimming pool would be reasonably more satisfied by 1,008 sides than by 4 sides. Further, I might then one day discover a book on geometry with a chapter on the 'circle' which would say what I would be saying about X, but on every occurrence of X would occur the word circle. Then to say: for 'X' read 'circle'. Now to the religious case.

2. In something of the same way, cosmic disclosures occur around models, and we might mark the objective reference of every cosmic disclosure, since there is only one individuation, by the symbol X. X would then be contextualized in the discourse which the generating model suggested, and in due course X would be contextualized in a multi-model discourse.

It might then happen that we chanced on a book of theology talking of God and love and purpose and activity and so on, father, shepherd, fisherman – indeed a Bible; and we might see that, on the one hand, so to say, where we read X, on the other hand we read the word God. We could then say again: for 'X' read 'God' – and in so far as the language fitted, to that degree we should necessarily talk of our cosmic disclosures as God.

I agree that the word 'God' by itself may seem of little use; unless it is contextualized it is a well-nigh empty name. But it is a useful way of pointing to the one cosmic individuation. In one sense when we have known the cosmic individuation, even on the first occasion, we have known God. But in another sense we have nearly everything to learn.

Let me conclude by turning round the question and ask: under what conditions, then, would God be merely a name for one way of looking at the world? Briefly my answer would be as follows:

1. If there is nothing in the world but its 'facts and features', or what are sometimes called 'states of affairs';

2. If talk about God's activity were only figurative and picturesque, e.g. saying of the thunder, God is angry today;

3. If cosmic disclosures were subjective experiences, or referred only to my peculiar way of looking at the world.

4. Further, it would be a poor way of looking at the world if theistic language were utterly incoherent, inconsistent and touched down nowhere on events in the world around us.

It is because I deny all these four assertions that I see belief in God as more than a particular way of looking at the world; but a reasonable way of talking about what discloses itself (himself) in a cosmic disclosure. To put the point more positively: to show that belief in God was more than an attitude to the world I said that we have first of all:

1. to defend a claim for transcendence;
2. to justify talk of God's activity;
3. to give an account of the reference of theological discourse;
4. to give some criteria for reasonable preference between alternative views of the universe – ways of looking at the world.

The claim for transcendence I justified first subjectively, and then by transference to the objective counterpart of a cosmic disclosure.

Talk of God's activity seemed to be justified because activity is a *logical primitive* – used of the objective referent of a cosmic disclosure as of ourselves because both match and meet.

This activity bearing on us, together with the claim for a single individuation (because the cosmic disclosure *is cosmic*), safeguards the reference.

Criteria for our discourse could be both logical and formal, and I then concluded by taking up the point which had been presupposed from the start: what entitles me to speak of what the cosmic disclosure discloses as God. I showed how there were ways of giving a reasonable answer here.

NOTES

1. Ronald Hepburn, 'The Gospel and the Claims of Logic', *Religion and Humanism*, BBC Publications 1964, p. 14.

2. Renford Bambrough, 'Homer and the Bishop of Woolwich', op. cit., p. 39.

3. Op. cit., p. 44.

4. Op. cit., p. 45.

5. Op. cit., p. 57.

6. Hymn 503, *Songs of Praise*, Enlarged Edition, Oxford University Press 1932.

7. *Songs of Praise*, 677 and 438.

8. Hepburn, op. cit., p. 16.

9. Ninian Smart, 'How Much Common Ground?', op. cit., pp. 92f.

BIBLIOGRAPHY OF THE PUBLISHED WORKS OF
IAN T. RAMSEY

Review of M. Farber, *The Foundation of Phenomenology: Edmund Husserl and the Quest for a Rigorous Science of Philosophy*, in *Cambridge Review*, Vol. LXVII, No. 1632, 17 Nov. 1945, p. 110

Review of D. M. Emmet, *The Nature of Metaphysical Thinking*, in *Cambridge Review*, Vol. LXVII, No. 1633, 24 Nov. 1945, p. 132.

Review of T. D. Weldon, *Introduction to Kant's Critique of Pure Reason*, in *Cambridge Review*, Vol. LXVII, No. 1640, 23 Feb. 1946, p. 273.

Review of W. A. Sinclair, *An Introduction to Philosophy*, in *Cambridge Review*, Vol. LXVII, No. 1643, 27 April 1946, p. 330.

Review of J. S. Lawton, *Conflict in Christology*, in *Theology*, Vol. LI, No. 335, May 1948, pp. 189–91.

'Man and Religion: Individual and Community', *Proceedings of the Tenth International Congress of Philosophy, August 1948*, Amsterdam 1949, pp. 308–10.

'Some Reflections on a Contemporary Problem Raised by Science and Religion', *Cambridge Journal*, Vol. II, No. 5, Feb. 1949, pp. 288–300.

University Sermon on 'Conversion', *Cambridge Review*, Vol. LXX, No. 1711, 26 Feb. 1949, pp. 437–39.

Review of Christopher Dawson, *Religion and Culture*, in *Cambridge Journal*, Vol. II, No. 11, Aug. 1949, pp. 694–96.

Hulsean Sermon, *Cambridge Review*, Vol. LXXII, No. 1751, 25 Nov. 1950, pp. 194f.

Review of J. Murphy, *The Origins and History of Religions*, in *Cambridge Journal*, Vol. IV, No. 4, Jan. 1951, pp. 245–47.

'Science and Religion' (BBC discussion with C. A. Coulson), *Church Pastoral Aid Society Fellowship Paper*, Vol. XIII, No. 149, May/June 1951, pp. 1–15.

Review of E. Cassirer, *The Problem of Knowledge*, in *Theology*, Vol. LIV, No. 377, Nov. 1951, pp. 433-35.

'Miracles: An Exercise in Logical Mapwork', Inaugural Lecture delivered in Oxford 7 Dec. 1951. Printed in *The Miracles and the Resurrection*, SPCK Theological Collections 3, London 1964, pp. 1-30.

Review of Christopher Dawson, *Religon and the Rise of Western Culture*, in *Cambridge Journal*, Vol. V, No. 7, April 1952, pp. 444-47.

'Joseph Butler (1752-1952)', *Oxford Magazine*, Vol. LXX, No. 24, 19 June 1952, pp. 394-97.

'The Challenge of Contemporary Philosophy to Christianity', *The Modern Churchman*, Vol. XLII, No. 3, Sept. 1952, pp. 252-269.

Review of F. F. Rigby, *Problems of Personal Relationships* and D. S. Bailey, *The Mystery of Love and Marriage* and *The Theology of Sex and Marriage*, in *Student Movement*, Oct. 1952, pp. 31-2.

'Notions and Ideas in Berkeley's Philosophy', *Proceedings of the Eleventh International Congress of Philosophy*, Amsterdam and Louvain 1953, Vol. XIII, pp. 66-71.

Review of J. Wisdom, *Philosophy and Psycho-analysis*, in *Oxford Magazine*, Vol. LXXII, No. 3, 29 Oct. 1953, pp. 52-4.

Sermon preached at the Festival Service in the chapel of Trinity College, Dublin, printed in *Hermathena*, No. LXXXII, Nov. 1953, pp. 113-27.

Review of C. E. Raven, *Natural Religion and Christian Theology*, *Cambridge Journal*, Vol. VIII, No. 3, Dec. 1953, pp. 189-90.

Discussion, 'Christianity and Lanaguage', *Philosophical Quarterly*, Vol. 4, No. 17, Oct. 1954, pp. 332-39.

Review of H. H. Farmer, *Revelation and Religion*, in *Cambridge Review*, Vol. LXXVI, No. 1846, 13 Nov. 1954, p. 175.

Review of F. H. Heinemann, *Existentialism and the Modern Predicament*, in *Hibbert Journal*, Vol. LIII, Jan. 1955, pp. 198-200.

Review of W. T. Stace, *Religion and the Modern Mind* and *Time and Eternity*, in *Mind*, Vol. LXIV, No. 253, Jan. 1955, pp. 110-12.

'The Systematic Elusiveness of "I"', *Philosophical Quarterly*, Vol. V, No. 20, July 1955, pp. 193-204.

Review of H. J. Paton, *The Modern Predicament*, in *Oxford Magazine*, Vol. LXXIV, No. 12, 9 Feb. 1956, pp. 260-1.

'Religion and Empiricism', *Cambridge Review*, Vol. LXXVII, No. 1879, 3 March 1956, pp. 404-5.

'Spiritual Healing', Central Society of Sacred Study, Leaflet 215, April 1956, pp. 15–26.

'The Paradox of Omnipotence', *Mind*, Vol. LXV, No. 258, April 1956, pp. 263–66.

'Cambridge by Birth; Oxford by Adoption', *Cambridge Review*, Vol. LXXVII, No. 1885, 19 May 1956, pp. 583–7.

'Empiricism and Religion', *The Christian Scholar*, Bloomfield, N. J., Vol. XXXIX, No. 2, June 1956, pp. 159–63.

'Persons and Funerals: What do Person Words Mean?', *Hibbert Journal*, Vol. LIV, No. 4, July 1956, pp. 330–38.

Review of E. E. Evans-Pritchard, *Nuer Religion*, in *Oxford Magazine*, Vol. LXXV, No. 10, 31 Jan. 1957, p. 244.

Review of *New Essays in Philosophical Theology*, ed. A. Flew and A. MacIntyre, in *Philosophical Quarterly*, Vol. 7, No. 27, April 1957, pp. 185–87.

'Ethics and Reason', *Church Quarterly Review*, Vol. 158, April 1957, pp. 153–60.

Religious Language: an Empirical Placing of Theological Phrases (Library of Philosophy and Theology), SCM Press, London, 1957.

'The Logical Character of Resurrection-belief', *Theology*, Vol. LX, No. 443, May 1957, pp. 186–92.

Review of M. B. Foster, *Mystery and Philosophy*, and B. Mitchell (ed.), *Faith and Logic*, in *Hibbert Journal*, Vol. LV, No. 4, July 1957, pp. 414–6.

Review of J. M. Todd, *The Springs of Morality*, in *Church Quarterly Review*, Vol. 158, July–Sept. 1957, pp. 364–66.

'Browne, 2. Sir Thomas', *Die Religion in Geschichte und Gegenwart*, Vol. I, 3rd ed., Tübingen 1957, cols. 1423–4.

Freedom and Immortality (the Forwood Lectures in the University of Liverpool, delivered in 1957), SCM Press, London, 1960.

Three articles for the *Telegu Encyclopaedia*, 1957.

Reviews of R. Hostie, *Religion and the Psychology of Jung*, and J. Pieper, *Justice*, in *Journal of Theological Studies*, NS Vol. VIII, No. 2, Oct. 1957, pp. 380–1, 413–14.

'The Two Moralities', *Journal of the William Temple Association*, Dec. 1957.

Review of D. M. MacKinnon, A Study in Ethical Theory, *View-Review*, Dec. 1957.

Review of R. Bultmann, *Primitive Christianity in its Contemporary Setting*, in *Philosophy*, Vol. XXXIII, No. 124, Jan. 1958, pp. 83–4.

Review of F. C. Happold, *Adventure in Search of a Creed*, in *Modern Churchman*, NS Vol. I, No. 3, Jan. 1958, pp. 201–2.

University Sermon, 'The Feast of Meeting', preached on 2 Feb. 1958, . printed in *Church Quarterly Review*, Vol. 160, Jan.–March 1959, pp. 11–20.

Reviews of Karl Barth, *Church Dogmatics* II, *The Doctrine of God*, Part 1, and R. Pieper, *Justice* and *The Science of St Thomas*, in *Modern Churchman*, NS Vol. I, No. 4, April 1958, pp. 254–6 and 258–259.

Review of H. A. Wolfson, *The Philosophy of the Church Fathers*, in *Philosophical Quarterly*, Vol. 8, No. 32, April 1958, pp. 186–8.

Review of R. L. Colie, *Light and Enlightenment*, in *Oxford Magazine*, Vol. LXXVI, No. 18, 8 May 1958.

'Deismus II: Begrifflich' and 'England III: Religionsphilosophie im 19 und 20 Jahrhunderten', *Die Religion in Geschichte und Gegenwart*, Vol. II, 3rd ed., Tübingen 1958, cols. 58–9, 486–91.

Editor, John Locke, *The Reasonableness of Christianity*, with *A Discourse of Morals* and part of *A Third Letter concerning Toleration*, A. & C. Black, London, 1958.

Review of H. F. Hallett, *Benedict de Spinoza*, in *Church Quarterly Review*, Vol. 159, Oct.–Dec. 1958, pp. 580–82.

Review of A. G. Wernham, *Benedict de Spinoza: The Political Works*, in *Journal of Theological Studies*, NS Vol. X, No. 1, April 1959, p. 229.

Review of W. M. Watt, *The Reality of God*, in *Philosophical Quarterly*, Vol. 9, No. 35, April 1959, p. 192.

Review of W. Burnett, *This is my Philosophy*, E. V. Sinnott, *Matter, Mind and Man*, and I. Leclerc, *Whitehead's Metaphyiscs*, in *Church Quarterly Review*, Vol. 160, July–Sept. 1959, pp. 399–401.

'Logical Empiricism and Patristics', delivered at the Third International Conference on Patristic Studies, Oxford, Sept. 1959, published in *Studia Patristica* V (Texte und Untersuchungen 80), Berlin 1962, pp. 451–7.

Review of M. Argyle, *Religious Behaviour*, in *Frontier*, Vol. 2, No. 3, Autumn 1959, pp. 219–20.

Review of J. S. Lawton, *Miracles and Revelation*, and H. D. McDonald, *Ideas of Revelation*, in *View-Review*, 1959.

'Paradox in Religion', *The Aristotelian Society, Supplementary Vol.* XXXIII, Harrison and Sons, London, 1959, pp. 195–218.

Review of *The Works of Jonathan Edwards: The Freedom of the Will*, ed. P. Ramsey, in *Philosophical Quarterly*, Vol. 9, No. 37, Oct. 1959, pp. 377–8.

Review of A. M. Farrer, *The Freedom of the Will*, in *Journal of Theological Studies*, NS Vol. X, No. 2, Oct. 1959, pp. 456–9.

Review of Ninian Smart, *Reasons and Faiths*, in *Philosophy*, Vol. 35, No. 321, Jan. 1960, pp. 86–88.

'Charles Darwin: *The Origin of Species*', *Leicester Cathedral Quarterly*, Vol. I, Nos. 1 and 2, Jan. and April 1960.

Review of F. H. Cleobury, *Christian Rationalism and Philosophical Analysis*, and W. F. Zuurdeeg, *An Analytical Philosophy of Religion*, in *Church Quarterly Review*, Vol. 161, July–Sept. 1960, pp. 355–357.

Review of John Wilson, *Language and Christian Belief* and *The Truth of Religion*, in *Philosophical Quarterly*, Vol. 10, No. 41, Oct. 1960, pp. 382–3.

'Contemporary Empiricism, its Development and Theological Implications', *The Christian Scholar*, Vol. XLIII, No. 3, Fall 1960, pp. 174–84.

Reviews of E. Coreth, O. Muck and J. Schasching, *Aufgaben der Philosophie*, and C. Cirne-Lima, *Der personale Glaube*, in *Journal of Theological Studies*, NS Vol. XI, No. 2, Oct. 1960, pp. 436–7.

Review of J. Heywood Thomas, *Subjectivity and Paradox: A Study of Kierkegaard*, in *Philosophy*, Vol. 35, No. 135, Oct. 1960, pp. 366–7.

Review of Karl Barth, *Church Dogmatics IV, The Doctrine of Reconciliation*, Part 2, in *Modern Churchman*, NS Vol. IV, No. 2, Jan. 1961, pp. 134–8.

'Religion and Science: A Philosopher's Approach', *Church Quarterly Review*, Vol. 162, Jan.–March 1961, pp. 77–91.

Review of G. Harland, *The Thought of Reinhold Niebuhr*, in *Oxford Magazine*, NS Vol. I, No. 19, 11 May 1961, pp. 342–3.

Review of J. Hartland-Swann, *An Analysis of Morals*, in *Church Quarterly Review*, Vol. 162, April–June 1961, pp. 228–9.

'Some Further Reflections on *Freedom and Immortality*', *Hibbert Journal*, Vol. LIX, No. 4, July 1961, pp. 348–55.

Review of A. C. Bridge, *Images of God*, in *Frontier*, Vol. 4, No. 3, Autumn 1961, pp. 216–17.

'History and the Gospels: Some Philosophical Reflections', delivered at the Second International Congress on New Testament Studies, Oxford, Sept. 1961, published in *Studia Evangelica* Vol. III, (Texte und Untersuchungen 88), Berlin 1964, pp. 201–17.

On Being Sure in Religion (F. D. Maurice Lectures for 1961), The Athlone Press, London, 1963.

Editor, *Prospect for Metaphysics: Essays of Metaphysical Exploration*, 1961. Introduction, pp. 7–11; 'On the Possibility and Purpose of a Metaphysical Theology', pp. 153–77.

'The Challenge of the Philosophy of Language', *London Quarterly and Holborn Review*, Vol. CLXXXVI, Oct. 1961, pp. 242–9.

'Frontiers of Christian Thought II: The Frontier of Philosophy', *Learning for Living*, Vol. I, No. 2, Nov. 1961, pp. 13–15.

Review of J. L. Moreau, *Language and Religious Language*, in *Church Quarterly Review*, Vol. 163, Jan.–March 1962, pp. 104–5.

Review of O. C. Thomas, *William Temple's Philosophy of Religion*, in *Oxford Magazine*, NS Vol. 2, No. 16, 15 March 1962, pp. 262–3.

Review of L. A. Reid, *Ways of Knowledge and Experience*, in *Journal of Theological Studies*, NS Vol. XIII, No. 1, April 1962, pp. 231–2.

Review of J. Wilson, *Philosophy and Religion: the Logic of Religious Belief*, in *Frontier*, Vol. 5, No. 3, Autumn 1962, pp. 528–9.

'Understanding your Faith: Truth and Religion', *London Churchman*, Oct. 1962.

Review of D. J. Elwood, *The Philosophical Theology of Jonathan Edwards*, in *Journal of Theological Studies*, NS Vol. XIII, No. 2, Oct. 1962, pp. 482–4.

Review of W. G. Maclagan, *The Theological Frontier of Ethics*, in *Mind*, Vol. LXXII, No. 286, April 1963, pp. 294–8.

The Alden-Tuthill Lectures on Theological Literacy: 1. 'On Understanding Mystery; 2. 'On Being Articulate about the Gospel; 3. 'A Logical Exploration of some Christian Doctrines', *Chicago Theological Seminary Register*, Vol. LIII, No. 5, May 1963.

Models and Mystery, Whidden Lectures for 1963, Oxford University Press, London, 1964.

Review of *Soundings: Essays concerning Christian Understanding*, ed. A. R. Vidler, in *Frontier*, Vol. 6, No. 2, Summer 1963, pp. 150–1.

Review of Karl Barth, *Church Dogmatics III, The Doctrine of Creation*, Parts 3–4, in *Modern Churchman*, NS Vol. VII, No. 3, April 1964, pp. 187–92.

Review of Karl Barth, *Church Dogmatics IV, The Doctrine of Reconciliation*, Part 3, in *Modern Churchman*, NS Vol. VII, No. 4, July 1964, pp. 243–7.

'Good Stewards of the Manifold Grace of God', *Christian Education*, July 1964, pp. 2–5.

'Towards the Relevant in Theological Language', *Modern Churchman*, NS Vol. VIII, No. 1, Oct. 1964, pp. 46–58.

Religion and Science, Conflict and Synthesis, SPCK, London, 1964; also in *Adult Teacher*, Tennessee, Vol. 19, No. 10, June 1966.

'A New Prospect in Theological Studies', *Theology*, Vol. LXVII, No. 534, Dec. 1964, pp. 527–33.

Editor, *Biology and Personality*, Basil Blackwell, Oxford, 1965. Introduction, pp. 1–8; 'Biology and Personality: some Philosophical Reflections', pp. 174–206.

'Discernment, Commitment and Cosmic Disclosures', *Religious Education*, Chicago, Vol. LX, No. 1, Jan–Feb. 1965.

Letter, 'The Intellectual Crisis of British Christianity', *Theology*, Vol. LXVIII, No. 536, Feb. 1965, pp. 109–11.

Reviews of A. A. Luce, *The Dialectic of Immaterialism*, and H. A. Meynall, *Sense, Nonsense and Christianity*, in *Journal of Theological Studies*, Vo.l XVI, No. 1, April 1965, pp. 267–70 and 270–1.

'Controversial Broadcasting and the Dialogue with Humanism', *The Christian Broadcaster*, July 1965.

'Het empirisme en de theologie', *Wending*, July –Aug. 1965.

Christian Discourse: Some Logical Exploration (Riddell Memorial Lectures, 35th Series), Oxford University Press, London, 1965.

'Charles Earle Raven, 1885–1964', *Proceedings of the British Academy*, Vol. 51, 1965, pp. 467–84.

'Contemporary Philosophy and the Christian Faith', *Religious Studies*, Vol. I, No. 1, Oct. 1965, pp. 47–61.

Review of G. W. H. Lampe and D. M. MacKinnon, *The Resurrection*, in *Mowbray's Journal*, No. 84, Autumn 1966, pp. 6–8.

Review of H. P. Owen, *The Moral Argument for Christian Theism*, in *Theology*, Vol. LXIX, No. 556, Oct. 1966, pp. 457–9.

'A Symposium on Christianity and Buddhism', *Japanese Religions*, Vol. 4, No. 2, 1966.

Editor, *Christian Ethics and Contemporary Philosophy* (Library of Philosophy and Theology), SCM Press, London, 1966. Discussion of R. Braithwaite, *An Empiricist's View of the Nature of Religious Belief,*' pp. 84–8;' Moral Judgments and God's Commands', pp. 152–71; 'Towards a Rehabilitation of Natural Law', pp. 382–396.

'Talking about God: Models, Ancient and Modern', in *Myth and Symbol*, ed. F. W. Dillistone, SPCK Theological Collections 7, London, 1966, pp. 76–97.

Review of W. I. Matson, *The Existence of God*, in *Journal of Philosophy*, New York, Vol. 64, No. 4, 2 March 1967, pp. 128–33.

'The Plowden Report', *Learning for Living*, Vol. 6, No. 5, May 1967, pp. 22–25.

Review of M. E. Marty, *Varieties of Unbelief*, and *Religion and Humanism* (Broadcast Talks by R. Hepburn and others), in *Frontier*, Vol. 10, No. 3, Autumn 1967, pp. 229–30.

Review of J. A. T. Robinson, *Exploration into God*, in *New Christian*, 2 Nov. 1967, p. 19.

'A Personal God', in *Prospect for Theology: Essays in Honour of H. H. Farmer*, ed. F. G. Healey, Nisbet, London, 1967, pp. 53–71.

Review of J. Macquarrie, *God-talk: An Examination of the Language and Logic of Theology*, in *Church Quarterly Review*, Vol. 169, Jan.–March, 1968, p. 111.

Review of T. McPherson, *The Philosophy of Religion*, in *Trivium*, Vol. III, May 1968, pp. 109–12.

'The Way Ahead for Christian Thinking', *Point*, Summer 1968.

'Polaayi and J. L. Austin', in *Intellect and Hope*, ed. T. A. Langford and W. H. Poteat, Duke University Press, Durham, N.C., 1968.

'Theology Today and Spirituality Today', in *Spirituality for Today*, ed. Eric James, SCM Press, London, 1968, pp. 74–86.

Review of P. Baelz, *Christian Thinking and Metaphysics* and *Prayer and Providence*, in *Church Quarterly*, Vol. 1, No. 2, Oct. 1968, pp. 170–1.

'Survey of Ethics: 1960–1966' in *Theological Book List*, Theological Education Fund of the World Council of Churches, 1968, pp. 56–63.

'Hell', in *Talk of God* (Royal Institute of Philosophy Lectures II, 1968–69), Macmillan, London, 1969, pp. 207–25.

'Pop and Revelation', *New Directions*, Vol. 1, No. 1, 1969.

'The Reasonableness of Faith Today', one of the Rochester Cathedral Lectures, 1969 (duplicated).

Joseph Butler, 1692–1752; Some Features of his Life and Thought (Friends of Dr Williams's Library Lecture 23), Dr Williams's Trust, London, 1969.

Opening Sermon at the Conference of Modern Churchmen, *Modern Churchman*, NS., Vol. XIII, No. 1, Oct. 1969, pp. 7–15.

'William Temple: Some Aspects of his Thought and Life', *Bishoprick*, Nov. 1969.

Review of H. Montefiore, *The Question Mark*, in *View-Review*, Vol. 20, No. 4, 1969.

Review of T. F. Torrance, *Theological Science*, in *The Times Literary Supplement*, 25 Dec. 1969, p. 1477.

'The Concept of the Eternal' in *The Christian Hope*, SPCK Theological Collections, No. 13, London 1970, pp. 35–48.

'Condemnation and Acceptance', *Burrswood Herald Quarterly*, 1970.

Review of W. Moberley, *The Ethics of Punishment*, in *Journal of Theological Studies*, NS Vol. XXI, No. 2, Oct. 1970, pp. 530–32.

Review of *Irish Anglicanism*, ed. M. Hurley, SJ, in *New Divinity*, Dublin, Vol. 1, No. 2, Nov. 1970, pp. 55–6.

'On Not Being Judgemental', *Bishoprick*, Nov. 1970.

'In Search of Absolute Moral Values' (a review of P. Roubiczek, *Ethical Values in the Age of Science*), in *The Times*, 21 Nov. 1970, p. 14.

Review of R. C. Miller, *The Language Gap and God: Religious Language and Christian Education*, in *Religious Education*, Chicago, Vol. LXV, No. 6, Nov.–Dec. 1970, pp. 524–8.

Review of K. Ward, *Ethics and Christianity*, J. Macquarrie, *Three Issues in Ethics*, and I. Trethowan, *Absolute Value*, in *Church Quarterly*, Vol. 3, No. 4, April 1971, pp. 333–6.

Review of T. F. Torrance, *God and Rationality*, in *The Spectator*, 10 April 1971.

Words about God: the Philosophy of Religion (Forum Books), SCM Press, London, and Harper, New York, 1971.

'Religion and Broadcasting', *The Brigade* (the magazine of the Church Lads' Brigade), Vol. LXXIX, No. 2, July 1971, pp. 6–7.

'The Influence of Technology on the Social Structure' (Trueman Wood Lecture), *Journal of the Royal Society of Arts*, Vol. CXIX, No. 5181, August 1971; also in *The Teilhard Review*, Vol. 6, No. 2, Winter 1971.

Our Understanding of Prayer (Archbishops' Commission on Christian Doctrine. Occasional Papers No. 1), SPCK, London, 1971.

Editor with Ruth Porter, *Personality and Science*, Churchill Livingstone, London, 1971.

Review of J. Morton, *Man, Science and God*, and A. R. Peacocke, *Science and The Christian Experiment*, in the *Guardian*, 17 Feb. 1972.

'Theology in England: Its Changing Face', *Escape*, Vol. 4, No. 6, May 1972.

'Crisis of Faith', An address to the Church Leaders' Conference, Birmingham, Sept. 1972. printed in *Theoria to Theory*, Vol. 7, No. 1, Jan. 1973, pp. 23–38.

'Northumbria', *The Methodist Conference, Newcastle-upon-Tyne*, 1973 *Handbook*, pp. 21–29.

INDEX

www.ingramcontent.com/pod-product-compliance
Lightning Source LLC
Chambersburg PA
CBHW071106090426
42737CB00013B/2506